# Humanistic Physical Education

*DONALD R. HELLISON*
Portland State University

PRENTICE-HALL, INC.
Englewood Cliffs, New Jersey

*Library of Congress Cataloging in Publication Data*

HELLISON, DONALD R.
    Humanistic physical education.

    Includes bibliographies.
    1. Physical education and training.    I. Title.
GV342.H44        613.7'07        73–1200
ISBN:   0–13–447789–8

© 1973 *Prentice-Hall, Inc.*
Englewood Cliffs, New Jersey

10   9   8   7   6   5   4   3   2   1

Printed in the United States of America

Prentice-Hall International, Inc., *London*
Prentice-Hall of Australia, Pty. Ltd., *Sydney*
Prentice-Hall of Canada, Ltd., *Toronto*
Prentice-Hall of India Private Limited, *New Delhi*
Prentice-Hall of Japan, Inc., *Tokyo*

# Contents

③

# Physical Education and Humanistic Goals:
## THE EVIDENCE                                                                    19

Introduction. Personality. Perceptions of Self and Body. Socially
Approved Behavior. Release of Tension, Anxiety, and Aggression.
Value Transfer. Leadership. Social Mobility. Sociometry.
Self-Actualization. Summary.

④

# Physical Education and the American Culture:
## CONSTRAINING FORCES                                                             39

Introduction. Cultural Values. *Sport and the culture. Cultural values.*
The Physical Education Profession. *Socialization. The physical educator's*
*value system. Factors responsible for the physical educator's value system.*
*Women physical educators. Summary.* Social Institutions. *The family.*
*Education. Government. Religion.* Minorities. *The disadvantaged. The*
*black athlete. Women in sport.*

⑤

# Prospects for Change                                                            67

Humanistic Physical Education. Mechanisms for Change. Signs of
Change. *Emergent values. The growth of humanism. Change in physical*
*education. Change in sport.* Summary.

## Methodology for Implementing
## a Humanistic Physical Education Program

Introduction. School Programs. Teaching Styles. Self-Esteem.
Self-Actualization. Self-Understanding. Interpersonal Relations.

Some people see things as they are
and say "Why?" I dream of things
that never were and say "Why not?"
*Robert F. Kennedy*

# *Preface*

This book represents a very personal effort to humanize physical education; there is nothing "value-free" about it. I have a vision for physical education and above all else I have tried to communicate this vision, elaborating each concept and proposition only to the point of understanding for the perspective being developed. Each topic—e.g., self-esteem, socialization, social change—suggests much more, but the rest is outside the scope of this book. Implicit in this vision is my own image of man; to a large extent whether my vision can be converted to reality depends upon whether it approximates man as he really is.

This book also reflects a personal struggle to resolve—or at least somehow juxtapose—two conflicting approaches to understanding: positivism, which, because it carries the aura of the scientific and the objective, seems so secure; and thought based upon subjective analyses of feelings, experiences, and observations.

My particular point of view must be placed in its proper perspective. The humanistic approach, an instrumental way of looking at physical education, is only one of what I consider to be a number of valid perspectives. For example, the argument that physical education has intrinsic value appears to have considerable merit. It is my opinion, however, that humanizing the conduct of physical education is long overdue and that this task is not diminished by the fact that physical education exists for reasons other than social and emotional well-being.

References appear at the end of each chapter. I have tried to cite everything which, to my knowledge, has influenced my thinking; the result is a mixture of primary and secondary as well as popular and scholarly sources. I have cited specific references in the body of the book sparingly.

Many sources which have been invaluable to me are not found in the references because they are experiences and people, not paper. The experiences are difficult to identify and cite; the people deserve mention here. First, my wife, Patsy, who has contributed to my growth in a hundred ways and to this work, especially Chapter six, materially. Second, my parents, who gave me a number of options early in life and whose sensitivity to human needs was extremely influential. Third, the many physical education majors and graduate students at Portland State and the students at Grant and Roosevelt High Schools in Portland who encouraged me to find another way and gave support when it was needed. Fourth, my teachers, who had an unwitting hand in this, especially F. Garvin Davenport of Monmouth College in Illinois, who taught me to do research; the late Jim Fleming of Kent State's sociology department; Ohio State's Sy Kleinman, who provoked me to thought and reflection; and Chalmer Hixson, whose insights into American athletics have been particularly helpful. Fifth, my friends and colleagues who have listened patiently and commented with insight on my ideas for the book, among them Ed Hubbell and Jim Hickey of the Marine Corps years, who were there at the beginning; Joe Willis, Dave Snyder, and Don Bethe during and after Ohio State; and the many Portland people, including Bob Olson, Bill White, and the Portland State physical education faculty—Milan, Maxine, the inspirational Ralph Davis, and others too numerous to mention here. Finally, my department head, Lee Ragsdale, who gave me the freedom and encouragement to complete this work.

# 1

# *Historical and Behavioral Perspectives*

## *Historical Perspective*

The primary objective of early physical education programs was, without a doubt, physical health. Even prior to the turn of the century, however, some American physical educators—especially Dudley Sargent, one of the most influential physical educators in recent history, and certain leaders of the German Turners and the YMCA—visualized a connection between physical education and social and emotional well-being. Their discussions of this relationship were vague, relying on speculation and personal observations for answers to questions of this nature. Not until after 1900, when sport became popular, did such outcomes as character development threaten to overshadow physical health as the major concern of physical education programs. By 1930, a new slogan—"education through the physical"—was employed by a group of physical educators led at first by Thomas Wood and Clark Hetherington, then by their students Jay B. Nash and Jesse F. Williams, and finally by Williams' student Delbert Oberteuffer. This slogan represented the belief that physical activity, particularly play and sport, provided the means to achieve nonphysical ends. It shifted the emphasis away from "education of the physical" and thereby caused an actively debated rift in the profession. Professional preparation programs began to reflect this new emphasis, particularly in courses such as "Principles of Physical Education," but the first major effort to analyze the sport-society relationship systematically was the book *Sport in American Life* [3] by Frederick Cozens and Florence Stumpf which did not appear until 1953.

Although some of the great names in sociology and psychology— Georg Simmel, Max Weber, George H. Mead, and William Graham Sumner, for example—intermittently studied and wrote about games, play, and leisure, these works, with the possible exception of Johan Huizinga's *Homo Ludens* [7], were not cited very much by physical educators; probably because they were either not read or not taken seriously. In fact, the collection of data and development of theory to support the increasing behavioral speculation by physical educators were conspicuous only by their absence until almost midcentury. There were a few early efforts, such as the measurement work by Luther Van Buskirk and Charles H. McCloy in the 1920s, but by the 1950s only Charles Cowell and a few others had contributed consistently to the literature. The 1960s, however, witnessed a proliferation in research, textbooks, college courses, conferences, and organizations concerned with the sociology and psychology of sport and exercise. Gerald Kenyon and one of his former students, John Loy, have been instrumental in conducting research, generating theory, organizing conferences, and, significantly, developing an alliance with sociologists interested in exploring sport-connected problems. Two organizations were formed to give continuity to this fast-growing speciality within physical education. The International Committee for the Sociology of Sport was organized in 1964 along cross-national lines; its journal, the *International Review of Sport Sociology,* provided a place for the publication of work from scholars of all nations who have an interest in sport sociology. Another organization, the North American Society for the Psychology of Sport and Physical Activity, was also formed to direct attention to and to improve communication among those interested in the area.

## The Need for a New Perspective

Several recent efforts have attempted to draw together behavioral theory, research, and speculation in the form of textbooks for physical educators by Peter McIntosh [15], Bryant J. Cratty [4], Celest Ulrich [21], and Peter Arnold [1] as well as collections of articles prepared by John Loy and Gerald Kenyon [12], George Sage [18], and Marie Hart [5]. These books have contributed to the profession's growing understanding of social and psychological processes. For the most part, they have adopted a value-free approach to the study of physical activity— that is, they have attempted to look at sport and exercise through disinterested, objective eyes. This reaction to the biases inherent in the "education through the physical" perspective has increased the dissemination of the body of knowledge usually labeled as sport sociology and psychology. Whether the conduct of physical education has been altered as a consequence of these books, however, is still undetermined. Although I have taken issue with the value-free approach elsewhere [6] and personally favor Lawrence Locke's point of view which stresses the development of theory and research applicable to the conduct of physical education [11], the expansion of the body of knowledge, however value-free, may be useful at a future date, particularly as the basis for applied work. There remains a need for a psychosocial textbook approach which has the conduct of physical education as a major concern. This book attempts to fill this need.

This book also has as its base a strong bias toward a humanistic point of view. Loosely translated, humanism means a concern for man above all else behaviorally and a concern for man's social and emotional well-being. Thus, there are many versions of humanism. Carl Weinberg argues that humanism resists classification:

> If we pause to indicate the precise nature of humanism, we will certainly not be performing a humanistic task, for we would be saying that humanism involves some standard prescription for defining itself and the tasks intending to represent it. Because humanism is an experience or perspective on life or education, it must define itself without a standard definition [23].

Thomas Robischon indicates that it seems strange even to talk about a humanistic education (or a humanistic physical education) for, after all, a concern for man is at the root of all educational functions [17]. Yet teachers behave many times as if students' feelings interfered with education, as if the subject matter would be contaminated by students as soon as they tried to come to grips with it. These priorities need to be reordered by applying humanistic goals to the subject matter of physical education.

At the risk of prescribing standards to which Weinberg has objected, I will briefly describe five of the major tenets of humanistic psychology in order to further clarify the concept of humanism. Humanistic psychology, which is often associated with encounter groups, sensitivity centers, and the like, has emerged as a "Third Force" in opposition to both Freudianism and behaviorism. The major tenets of this view are as follows: (1) Man's major goal in life is to actualize his own potentialities, to become all that he can become, to attain the status of the fully functioning person. Instead of the absence of sickness (negative), psychological health involves for him a high level "wellness" (positive). (2) Each individual has unique potentialities; no two people are the same in needs, abilities, or interests. As such, there is no justification for molding students into some predetermined shape. (3) Individuals must develop a "selective detachment" from their culture in order to avoid mirroring the values of society and thereby inhibiting individual development. (4) How a person feels is more important than what he knows; in fact, how he feels about himself (his self-esteem) and about what he is supposed to be learning will determine whether he will learn anything. Further, individuals with self-esteem difficulties will not be able to strive toward self-actualization to any extent. (5) No one is better able, at least potentially, than the person himself to determine how he best learns and what is most meaningful for him to learn.

## Concepts

For the purpose of this book I have divided physical education into programs of physical education and patterns of physical activity. *Programs of physical education* refer to any organized effort to structure learning or development which focuses on large muscle physical performance over a specified period of time. These programs include both in- and out-of-school programs ranging from individual motor learning lessons for a mentally retarded child to adult fitness programs; they exclude (1) recreation programs and sport programs in which learning or development is not a planned experience, and (2) "one shot" tournaments, meets, matches, games, and concerts. *Patterns of physical activity* refer to those large muscle physical activities that people typically engage in outside of physical education programs. The active games that children regularly play, such as tether ball, and the trend toward widespread adult jogging are examples of physical activity patterns which exist outside of physical education programs. Patterns of physical activity can also refer to those activities that a specific individual regularly engages in, such as tennis or a home fitness routine.

The term *physical ability*, as it is used throughout this book, refers to competency in a wide range of components of large muscle activity —from components usually associated with fitness, such as strength and aerobic capacity, to performance-oriented components such as speed, balance, and specific sport skills.

Chapters two and three describe the potential contributions of physical education programs and participation in physical activities to social and emotional well-being. Chapter two describes four humanistic goals, and Chapter three provides an overview of the evidence related to those goals. Chapter four describes those forces—cultural values, social institutions, minority status, and the physical education profession—which have prevented both programs and patterns from contributing more to humanistic goals. Chapter five contrasts the potentialities with the realities, describes mechanisms for social change, and discusses the prospects for change. Finally, Chapter six describes the methodology for implementing humanistic goals in physical education, and Chapter seven summarizes the major points and themes of the book.

# References

1. Arnold, Peter. *Education, Physical Education, and Personality Development.* New York: Atherton Press, Inc., 1968.
2. Cowell, Charles C. "The Contributions of Physical Activity to Social Development." *Research Quarterly,* XXXI (May 1960), 286–306.
3. Cozens, Frederick W., and Stumpf, Florence S. *Sports in American Life.* Chicago: University of Chicago Press, 1953.
4. Cratty, Bryant J. *Social Dimensions of Physical Activity.* Englewood Cliffs, N.J.: Prentice-Hall, Inc., 1967.
5. Hart, M. Marie, ed. *Sport in the Socio-Cultural Process.* Dubuque: William C. Brown Company, Publishers, 1972.
6. Hellison, Donald R. "Hellison's Reaction to 'The Nature of Sociological

Theory and its Importance for the Explanation of Agonetic Behavior.'" *Proceedings of the National College Physical Education Association for Men,* LXXIV (December 1970), 109–10.

7. Huizinga, Johan. *Homo Ludens: A Study of the Play Element in Culture.* Boston: Beacon Press, 1955.

8. Kelley, Earle C. "The Place of Affective Learning." *Educational Leadership* XXII (April 1965), 455–57.

9. Kroll, Walter P. *Perspectives in Physical Education.* New York: Academic Press, Inc., 1971.

10. Lewis, Guy M. "Adoption of the Sports Program, 1906–39: The Role of Accommodation in the Transformation of Physical Education." *Quest,* XII (May 1969), 34–46.

11. Locke, Lawrence F. *Research in Physical Education.* New York: Teachers College Press, 1969.

12. Loy, John W., Jr., and Kenyon, Gerald S., eds. *Sport, Culture, and Society.* New York: The Macmillan Company, 1969.

13. Martindale, Don. *The Nature and Types of Sociological Theory.* Boston: Houghton Mifflin Company, 1960.

14. Maslow, Abraham H. *Motivation and Personality.* 2nd ed. New York: Harper & Row, Publishers, 1970.

15. McIntosh, Peter C. *Sport in Society.* London: Watts, 1963.

16. Oberteuffer, Delbert, and Ulrich, Celeste. *Physical Education.* 3rd ed. New York: Harper & Row, Publishers, 1962.

17. Robischon, Thomas. "Philosophy and Education." In *Humanistic Foundations of Education,* edited by Carl Weinberg, pp. 11–40. Englewood Cliffs, N.J.: Prentice-Hall, Inc., 1972.

18. Sage, George H., ed. *Sport and American Society.* Reading, Mass.: Addison-Wesley Publishing Co., Inc., 1970.

19. Scott, M. Gladys. "The Contributions of Physical Activity to Psychological Development." *Research Quarterly,* XXXI (May 1960), 307–20.

20. Sloan, William W. "Education for Health." Division of Health and Physical Education, Wayne State University, June 15, 1964. Dittoed.

21. Ulrich, Celeste. *The Social Matrix of Physical Education.* Englewood Cliffs, N.J.: Prentice-Hall, Inc., 1968.

22. Van Dalen, Deobold B., Mitchell, Elmer D., and Bennett, Bruce L. *A World History of Physical Education.* Englewood Cliffs, N.J.: Prentice-Hall, Inc., 1953.

23. Weinberg, Carl. "Introduction." In *Humanistic Foundations of Education,* edited by Carl Weinberg, pp. 1–10. Englewood Cliffs, N.J.: Prentice-Hall, Inc., 1972.

24. Weinberg, Carl, and Reidford, Philip. "Humanistic Educational Psychology." In *Humanistic Foundations of Education,* edited by Carl Weinberg, pp. 101–32. Englewood Cliffs, N.J.: Prentice-Hall, Inc., 1972.

# 2

# Physical Education and Humanistic Goals:

## THEORETICAL CONSIDERATIONS

## Self-Esteem

Although social and emotional well-being refers to a broad range of concepts from personality traits to interpersonal relations, the self is central to most if not all of these concepts. An individual develops a "self-other" awareness at an early age, a distinction which enables each person to reflect on his own behavior and to be both the subject ("*I* can do it") and the object ("It happened to *me*") of his own action. It is this conscious awareness of himself, developed as he becomes aware of his relations to others, that distinguishes man from lower forms of life. The self is not only unique to man; it also plays a central role in man's needs and goals. Man strives to achieve self-esteem and self-actualization [15], to continually upgrade his own adequacy to cope with life [4], to be competent [28], to avoid anxiety [1]. William Purkey summarizes the various strands of thought by stating that all human behavior is motivated by a desire to maintain and enhance the self [19].

Gerald Kenyon has suggested that the self takes its interpretation —actual self, perceived self, or ideal self—from the personality theory —clinical, experimental, or social psychological—underlying it [10]. This chapter is oriented toward the perceived self described by Arthur Combs and Donald Snygg as "Not only a person's physical self but everything he experiences as 'me' at that instant," including his appearance, abilities, limitations, and relations with others as he views them [4]. These cognitive and emotional experiences form the basis for those beliefs which the individual holds to be true about himself. Different beliefs are developed for each ability or role that the individual perceives to be a part of himself; for example, a teen-age boy will hold different beliefs about himself as student, friend, athlete, son, and auto mechanic. Each of these beliefs has a corresponding value; the same boy may highly value being an athlete but give his student role a lower priority. Further, these beliefs and values may not correlate well; he may believe that he is not very competent at the particular role or ability which he highly values (such as playing baseball), or he may believe that he is very good at a role or ability which is not important to him (such as getting good grades). Finally, these beliefs influence behavior; if he believes that he is not very good at a particular task (jumping hurdles), he will perform in accordance with these beliefs (avoid performing in this event) which in turn reinforces the belief that he is not very good.

Many of us have the mistaken impression that we build our self-perceptions from fact rather than from beliefs derived from highly subjective interpretations of our own experiences. Nowhere is this clearer than in competitive sport, in which the scoreboard has been consecrated as the supreme "factual" evaluator of all physical performance. Yet if I as coach or performer select my opponents carefully, or if I as a performer compete in a weak league or conference, or if I as an informal participant am never exposed to excellence in a particular activity, then the scoreboard has not really evaluated me objectively. Furthermore, this seems to be healthy if we are concerned with positive self-esteem, because by objective standards of performance only a few would succeed against stronger opponents—the professional and Olympic athletes, for example—while everyone else would experience failure. Instead, we all develop our own subjective criteria for what it takes to be "great" or "good" or "mediocre" or "a failure." An Olympic athlete may evaluate himself as inadequate, while a neighborhood softball player may see himself as a "star." The subjectivity of these criteria is in part explained by each individual's uniquely developed frame of reference which uses past experiences, both cognitive and emotional, to filter all perceptions. Another partial explanation involves cognitive defenses which aid people in evaluating themselves in the most favorable light. These defenses, sometimes referred to as self-deception and self-justification, permit the individual to manipulate the facts—to ignore some and reinterpret others—with the goal of a positive self-evaluation. The end result is a tendency toward a revision upward of answers to the question "Who am I?"

A different explanation of this phenomenon, known as level of aspiration theory, differentiates among the goals to which individuals aspire in relation to their ability. This approach emphasizes objective success or failure to achieve a specific goal—such as first place in a local tournament—which, in turn, affects future goals, evaluations of the probability of success in related goals, and self-evaluation. What is not accounted for is the impact of winning or losing that tournament, for example, on the individual's perceptions of becoming "good" or "great." The same tournament result may have significantly different effects, depending upon the individual's subjective criteria for performance. His level of aspiration may be influenced so that, for example, he will not enter a more prestigious tournament after losing in a local affair; however, he may still evaluate himself as a "good" and "worthy" performer who is in the eightieth percentile of all regular players or he may think of himself as a "loser" who is in the tenth percentile. Neither evaluation may resemble the truth of the matter, because factors other than that tournament result and past tournament results shape his perceptions of his physical ability and subsequently his self-esteem as a performer.

These beliefs (self-perceptions) are related to self-esteem—how an individual feels about himself in terms of direction (positive/negative) and intensity (how positive or negative)—and reflect the extent of his approval or disapproval of himself. This definition allows us to focus attention on an individual's private evaluation of his competence in performing a specific task or role rather than on the various beliefs he holds to be true about himself or hopes he has for himself. Whereas self-perceptions refer to all of an individual's beliefs about himself based on past experiences, self-esteem refers to the individual's personal evaluation of those beliefs.

Every person develops a specific self-esteem for each specific ability or role that he perceives himself to perform based on his perceptions of that ability or role. Everyone may also possess a generalized self-esteem derived from some summation of these specific self-esteems, but the concept of an overall self-evaluation has yet to be proven and is therefore still a matter for speculation. If such a concept exists, it refers to positive or negative feelings about the self in general as represented by the statement "At times I feel no good at all."

The potential impact of physical education or any other effort on self-esteem, whether specific or general, would be severely limited if self-esteem were not amenable to change. Fortunately, it appears that self-esteem can be changed even in adulthood. Self-evaluations of a particular role or ability are apparently considerably less difficult to modify than generalized self-esteem, if such a concept exists. A person can more easily raise or lower his self-esteem as a gymnast, for example, than he can his overall view of himself. These specific self-evaluations are modified by perceptions of success and failure, and there is some experimental evidence [5] that spill-over of one kind of self-esteem to another can occur, especially if change is observed in an ability or role that is highly valued. If an individual improves his feelings about his ability to swim, which he highly values, his evaluation of his ability to relate to his friends may also improve. The social environment, particularly "significant others" in a person's life, can alter self-esteem if he perceives changes in the behavior of significant others toward him, as in the coach's effort to bolster one of his players by paying attention to the positive aspects of his play. It should be made clear that self-esteem change is a complex matter which also involves other factors such as conceptual differentiation, consistency, and salience.

Physical education programs and physical activity patterns provide the setting within which an individual develops perceptions of his physical performance in a specific activity or of his general physical ability. These perceptions in turn constitute the basis for his evaluation of his physical self or, more accurately, of his physical ability self. His self-esteem is the result of the direction and intensity of his feelings about his perceptions of his performance or ability, taking such forms as "I am a good athlete" or "I am ashamed of the awkward way I move." If an individual's perceptions of his ability change, his self-esteem in relation to that ability will also shift. Further, changes in physical ability self-esteem may lead to changes in other self-evaluations (such as social

ability or academic ability) if physical ability is highly val
individual.

Although many programs other than physical education c
alter an individual's self-esteem, there are at least three reasons for
suggesting that physical education should receive special consideration
in any discussion of self-esteem change. First, the American culture has
traditionally extolled the value of physical prowess, fitness, and appearance. It is difficult for the growing boy, for example, to disregard physical ability in his private value system, no matter what his talents or
limitations. Second, perceptions of the body and self-perceptions paral-
lel each other according to experimental evidence [31] as well as theoretical propositions [9, 18]. The implication is that activities which
primarily involve the body will affect self-perceptions. Research bear-
ing on this question is reviewed in Chapter three. Third, physical education has a highly visible affective dimension. As the psychologist Arthur
Jersild points out, everyone comes out of the physical education experience feeling better or worse, never neutral [3]. Simon Wenkart,
explaining man's involvement in physical activity, states that physical
activity gives the "awkward and self-conscious . . . the feeling of being-
in-the-world," [27] again stressing the affective component of our subject matter.

Since self-esteem change has been associated with the influence of
"significant others," a brief examination of physical education's role in
providing those significant others is in order. (The next chapter indirectly explores this topic by looking at the physical educator as a socializing agent in the transfer of values from sport to society.) While
exposure to the usual number and range of social stimuli in a person's
life prevents any one individual other than parents from making much
of an impact, at least three factors enhance the possibility of physical
educators becoming significant others for some individuals: (1) the prestige and power of the socializing agent, for example, a popular coach;
(2) the value assigned to certain athletic programs by the culture; (3) the
extent of voluntary, intense involvement by the participant, as in competitive sport. One limitation of these hypothesized factors is that they
are only applicable for the most part to a specific kind of physical
education program (namely interscholastic athletics for boys) whose
participants are often already high in self-esteem, sometimes to the
point of arrogance. It may be that encouragement and positive rein-
forcement from these coaches in other kinds of programs would be
beneficial to individuals with low self-esteem, but this is conjectural at
present.

To review briefly, it has been suggested that self-awareness is developed in all societies, that the self is central to man's basic needs and lifetime goals, that an individual's perception of himself and particularly the extent to which he likes or dislikes himself greatly influences his behavior, that each individual develops a self-esteem for every ability or role that he perceives himself to have in the society and that each of these abilities has a different value attached to it, that self-esteem in relation to these abilities can be altered, and that a change in a highly valued self-esteem could cause other self-esteems to change. The case for physical education's importance in the process of self-esteem development has rested on several factors: (1) physical ability and physical appearance are valued in the American culture; (2) physical education has a visible affective component; (3) the body and self are related; (4) an individual's evaluation of his physical ability is based on subjective perceptions which can be altered, leading to self-esteem change; (5) physical education has a unique, although limited, potential for providing significant others who can influence the self-esteem of participants in certain physical education programs.

What we have here, it seems, are three concepts—i.e., self-perception, self-esteem, and physical education—depicted in a series of causal relationships—i.e., self-esteem change depends on what happens to self-perceptions which are in turn influenced by physical education programs and, to a lesser extent, patterns of activity. Loy's distinction between what is and what is not theory warns against labeling something as theory which does not meet the criteria of generality, formalization, and testability [14]. Clearly this is only a set of propositions which needs to be validated by evidence. Unfortunately, as the next chapter demonstrates, many of these relationships have not been examined.

An individual's self-esteem is a very important beginning, because it forms the base of support for behavioral development. Even if self-esteem is specific to ability or role and spill-over to other abilities or roles is minimal, a person's base of support is widened every time he increases his feelings of competence about a particular motor skill, physical activity, or capability of his body.

## Self-Actualization

As important as self-esteem development is in influencing one's behavior, Abraham Maslow's theory of motivation only views self-esteem as a prerequisite to growth toward self-actualization [15]. Maslow's description of self-actualization refers to "the full use and exploitation of talents, capacities, potentialities, etc." which presumably includes physical abilities as well as other kinds, although Maslow pays more attention to such qualities as acceptance of self and others, spontaneity, detachment, autonomy, creativity, and interpersonal relations. Yet his later references to the potentialities of art and music in the curriculum [16] suggest that the development of the performing arts (of which sport is a part) is one dimension of self-actualization.

It appears that Maslow's theory that self-esteem development precedes good growth toward self-actualization could apply to physical education as well. For Maslow, perceptions of reality of self-actualized people differ from those of others in that they more nearly approximate reality. If physical education's first task was self-esteem development, at least within the narrow confines of physical activity, a secondary goal could be a full realization of each individual's unique physical potentials and with it the development of more realistic perceptions of individual abilities. In other words, facing reality is not nearly so difficult for someone who finds himself learning what makes him unique and then developing as fully as he is able these potentialities.

Self-actualization in this view means the identification and development of specific physical abilities in line with an individual's potentialities. Everyone's potential talents span a wide range of abilities including those within the province of physical education; therefore, everyone can become self-actualized in physical education if these unique talents are developed. This development may be a lifelong process, or it may occur early in life and become part of the individual's special memories.

According to this view, physical ability development is the major contribution of physical education to self-actualization. However, there are at least two other potential contributions: the creative, self-expressive function of movement, and the feelings and meanings associated with total involvement in physical performance. Humanistic psychology has attached considerable importance to the cultivation of both creativity and the ability to express one's self fully as components of the "authentic person," and to:

> the existential "here and now" moment of beingness, well-beingness, aliveness and full humanness; awareness and full utilization of one's sensory existence; [and] innovative, experimental, experiential forms and processes free from more conventional institutional limitations. [2]

Probably the best examples of creative self-expression in physical education within the American culture are modern dance and movement
exploration. The other potential contribution, total involvement in
physical performance, refers to those feelings and meanings that a performer attaches to a particular performance when he is immersed in it.
These feelings and meanings are difficult to describe specifically, but the
following personal description of one person's experience exemplifies
total involvement:

> You start to feel the tremendous friction caused by the unbelievable
> speed at which you travel around the bar. Your hands are aching; the
> bar tears and rips at them. You must hold on. They burn now; your
> hands are trying to shed an unwanted annoyance. But you must hold
> on. . . . The ceiling trades places with the floor; then the floor with the
> ceiling. And then very abruptly and seemingly miraculously, you find
> yourself standing on your feet. You feel like you have transgressed
> into one exciting world and then back again. You feel wonderful. You
> cannot name what that feeling is, but it does not matter. As long as
> it is there, you will keep returning to that world. [12]

According to Daryl Siedentop, this kind of total involvement comes
very close to Maslow's description of the peak experience and Carl
Rogers' conceptualization of the fully functioning person [23].

## Self-Understanding

A healthy self-perception provides a sound foundation for becoming what one is capable of becoming, and the identification and development of one's unique abilities and feelings build a substantial
structure upon this foundation. The next step is the integration of these
feelings and abilities into a meaningful life style. Accomplishing this
task requires an understanding of one's self, of one's abilities, interests,
and needs as well as the causes of these variables. Does the individual
have a need to win in any competitive situation? Why does he possess
this need? Does he possess a creative inclination? To what extent do the
interests and abilities he has cultivated meet his needs? Remembering
that growth toward actualization of a person's physical potentialities
probably improves the accuracy of physical ability self-perceptions, it
is nevertheless common to observe a kind of blind development of
individual talents without corresponding guidance into the ways in

which these talents can be blended into a life style. Probably just as often we see those individuals who seemingly cannot compete casually in, say, backyard badminton, who view modern dance as an effeminate activity, or who have difficulty accepting certain physical limitations. All of these examples and many more can profit from guidance which encourages introspection by the individual into the relationship between physical education and his life.

Introspection of this nature is painful, if not impossible, unless both positive self-esteem and at least some development of individual abilities are present; but, given these characteristics, an individual may be willing and able to attempt self-analysis of that ability or role which he has both evaluated positively and developed to some extent. He can then bring his needs into focus and deal with them in relation to his abilities and interests. An example of this process is the individual who has a need to become a great athlete. Ideally, the development of both his abilities and his perceptions of his worth as a performer would reduce this need, but introspection with an eye toward meeting this need in the future, for instance through participation in local leagues or tournaments, might prevent him from forcing this need on his children as he observes and guides them in sport in their early years.

Applying this process to physical education, program objectives would include not only self-esteem and the development of physical potentialities, but also guidance, having as its goal introspection into the connection between the individual's physical abilities, needs, and interests, and his life. Ideally, his future patterns of physical activity would be based on decisions made at this time and modified in accordance with new information and the ongoing introspective process.

## Interpersonal Relations

It should be clear that our overriding emphasis so far has been the potential contributions which physical education can make to psychological well-being. Once this process is under way, attention can be turned to social considerations. Society comprises a complex network of person-to-person and group-to-group relationships which are all too often characterized by prejudice, intolerance, and ignorance. Although positive self-esteem, the development of individual abilities, and life style introspection no doubt aid in the development of healthy interpersonal relations by reducing anxieties, doubts, and defensive behavior, physical education's contribution to this process is no guarantee that interpersonal relations will be affected. If physical education is to have an impact on interpersonal relations, it must emphasize the value of such qualities as cooperation and sensitivity toward others.

The tradition of physical education is heavily sprinkled with claims that sport in particular promotes two rather opposite kinds of values: sportsmanship and cooperation, on one hand, and survival-of-the-fittest values such as achievement and discipline, on the other. These values are not really at opposite poles unless sport's interaction process is subverted by the war-oriented "win-at-all (or most) costs" approach, but in any case neither of these kinds of values (i.e., diffuse roles) automatically derive from sport nor are they readily transferred into nonsport situations, as the next chapter will discuss. It appears that programs of physical education and particularly sport do hold great promise for the teaching of values, both because sport is, in Ulrich's words, "the epitome of interaction" [25] and because sport has a built-in highly visible affective component—that is, it is difficult not to feel better or worse as the result of the experience.

In order to inculcate a value in sport and cause it to be transferred into nonsport situations, Thomas Sheehan and William Alsop have developed a concept of educational sport [22]. In their view, instruction concerning a specific value follows skills and strategy instruction for a particular sport. The value under consideration is discussed at length as it appears in the sport. Then, scrimmages are held wherein play is interrupted to point out where the value has been applied or ignored. Finally, follow-up lectures and discussions are held which focus on the application of the value to nonsport situations. An alternative approach which is particularly applicable to games and relays for youngsters involves observation of the extent of cooperation and sensitivity toward others exhibited during the activity followed by a discussion of what happened and why in relation to these values.

Mario Fantini and Gerald Weinstein have argued for a three-tiered approach to all education [6]. In their model, the third tier is exclusively devoted to learning about interpersonal relations outside of the traditional disciplines, with particular emphasis on sensitivity toward others. If this emphasis and at least some of the objectives and methods described by Fantini and Weinstein could be combined with Sheehan's educational sport concept or some derivative, programs of physical education would further increase their potential for aiding human development.

But an isolated program touching someone's life only briefly and intermittently cannot hope to achieve any of the objectives described in this chapter, although some faint sense of good feelings and somewhat better performance may result. Instead, it seems necessary to systematically develop a wide-ranging interrelated set of programs which touches its participants year after year, not only in physical education but in other areas as well. Whether this is within the realm of possibility is the subject of Chapter five.

# References

1. Becker, Ernest. *The Birth and Death of Meaning.* New York: The Free Press, 1962.
2. Caldwell, Stratton F. "The Human Potential Movement: Origin, Emergence and Relationship to the Field of Physical Education." Paper presented at CAHPER Conference, Oakland, California, April 1–6, 1971. Dittoed.
3. Cogan, Max. "Creative Approaches to Physical Education." *Proceedings of the National College Physical Education Association for Men,* LXXIII (December 1969), 131–38.
4. Combs, Arthur W., and Snygg, Donald. *Individual Behavior: A Perceptual Approach to Behavior.* Rev. ed. New York: Harper & Row, Publishers, 1959.
5. Diggory, J.C. *Self-Evaluation: Concepts and Studies.* New York: John Wiley & Sons, Inc., 1966.
6. Fantini, Mario, and Weinstein, Gerald. *Making Urban Schools Work: Social Realities and the Urban School.* New York: Holt, Rinehart and Winston, Inc., 1968.
7. Gergen, Kenneth J. *The Concept of Self.* New York: Holt, Rinehart and Winston, Inc., 1971.
8. Jersild, Arthur T. *In Search of Self.* New York: Teachers College Press, 1952.
9. Johnson, Warren R. "Some Psychological Aspects of Physical Rehabilitation: Toward an Organismic Theory." *Journal of the Association for Physical and Mental Rehabilitation,* XVI (November 1962), 165–68.
10. Kenyon, Gerald S. "Attitude toward Vertiginous Physical Activity as a Function of Self-and Body-Esteem." Paper presented at Research Section, AAHPER, Las Vegas, March 12, 1967. Mimeographed.
11. Kenyon, Gerald S. "Sociological Considerations." *JOHPER,* XXXIX (November 1968), 31–33.
12. Kleinman, Seymour. "Toward a Non-Theory of Sport." *Quest,* X (May 1968), 29–34.
13. Lippman, Walter. "The World Outside and the Pictures in Our Heads." In *Images of Man: The Classic Tradition in Sociological Thinking,* edited by C. Wright Mills, pp. 21–47. New York: George Brazziller, Inc., 1960.
14. Loy, John W. "The Nature of Sociological Theory and Its Importance for the

Explanation of Agonetic Behavior." *Proceedings of the National College Physical Education Association for Men,* LXXIV (December 1970), 94–105.

15. Maslow, Abraham H. *Motivation and Personality.* 2nd ed. New York: Harper & Row, Publishers, 1970.

16. Maslow, Abraham H. "Peak Experiences in Education and Art." *Humanist,* XXXI (March/April 1971), 6–11.

17. Mosston, Muska, and Mueller, Rudy. "Mission, Omission, and Submission in Physical Education." *Proceedings of the National College Physical Education Association for Men,* LXXIII (December 1969), 122–30.

18. Oberteuffer, Delbert, and Ulrich, Celeste. *Physical Education.* 3rd ed. New York: Harper & Row, Publishers, 1962.

19. Purkey, William. *Self Concept and School Achievement.* Englewood Cliffs, N.J.: Prentice-Hall, Inc., 1970.

20. Rosenberg, Morris. *Society and the Adolescent Self-Image.* Princeton, N.J.: Princeton University Press, 1965.

21. Shaver, Phillip. "Measurement of Self-Esteem and Related Constructs." In *Measures of Social-Psychological Attitudes,* edited by John P. Robinson and Phillip R. Shaver, pp. 45–69. Ann Arbor: Institute for Social Research, 1969.

22. Sheehan, Thomas J., and Alsop, William L. "Educational Sport." *JOHPER,* XLIII (May 1972), 41–45.

23. Siedentop, Daryl. *Physical Education: Introductory Analysis.* Dubuque: William C. Brown Company, Publishers, 1972.

24. Smith, M. Brewster. "Competence and Socialization." In *Socialization and Society,* edited by John A. Clausen, pp. 270–320. Boston: Little, Brown and Company, 1968.

25. Ulrich, Celeste. *The Social Matrix of Physical Education.* Englewood Cliffs, N.J.: Prentice-Hall, Inc., 1968.

26. Vanek, M., and Cratty, Bryant J. *Psychology and the Superior Athlete.* London: The Macmillan Company, 1970.

27. Wenkart, Simon. "The Meaning of Sports for Contemporary Man." *Journal of Existential Psychiatry,* III (Spring 1963), 397–404.

28. White, R. W. "Motivation Reconsidered: The Concept of Competence." *Psychological Review,* LXVI (1959), 297–333.

29. Wylie, Ruth C. *The Self-Concept.* Lincoln: University of Nebraska Press, 1961.

30. Ziller, Robert C. *et al.* "Self-Esteem: A Self-Social Construct." *Journal of Consulting and Clinical Psychology,* XXXIII (February 1969), 1969), 84–95.

31. Zion, Leela C. "Body-Concept as It Relates to Self-Concept." *Research Quarterly,* XXXVI (December 1965), 490–95.

# 3

# Physical Education and Humanistic Goals:

## THE EVIDENCE

## Introduction

Humanism is often accused of being mystical, antiscientific, or at best philosophical and therefore not amenable to proof or "hard data" research. However, research in physical education has focused on psychological and social outcomes of the physical education experience, and the results shed some light on the feasibility of humanistic goals.

Although research literature overflows with studies of the relationship between physical education programs and psychosocial and sociological variables, there are at least three serious difficulties in utilizing the studies to validate the wide range of social and psychological benefits often claimed as outcomes of physical education programs. First, cross-sectional studies in which data are gathered only once do not indicate whether change has occurred. Longitudinal investigations which gather data both before a program begins and after it ends are more likely to provide an adequate basis for assessing the contributions of physical education to individual development. Second, the question of whether a change has occurred is compounded by the multitude of factors which comprise any physical education program. The type of activity, sex and age level of the participants, number and frequency of exposures to the activity, characteristics of the teacher, and teaching methods are all at least potentially involved in the change. Sometimes a particular study will attempt to isolate the factors under investigation, but many times the effects of the various factors remain obscure. Third, the validity of psychosocial and sociological measurement techniques is often suspect; in many cases little consensus has been achieved concerning which tool to use to measure a particular variable in a particular situation. For example, some have argued that instruments designed to measure self-concept or self-esteem are really self-reports which only reveal what the individual is willing to disclose. In recognition of these methodological deficiencies, the strategy employed in this chapter has been to concentrate on those studies which have investigated change and to emphasize caution in the interpretation of the often highly tentative conclusions drawn here. From time to time references are made to literature which departs somewhat from a research orientation in order to clarify a particular concept and to help fill gaps as yet untouched by research. The recent proliferation of research in the social and psychosocial aspects of sport and exercise should eventually close these gaps, thereby relegating this chapter to the growing collection of out-of-date physical education literature.

The research studies in this chapter are organized so that those which have the self as a primary referent appear first, followed by a review of those studies which are concerned with interpersonal relations. The self-other relationship is often central to this latter group of studies. A brief review of evidence regarding physical development has also been included in deference to the self-actualization discussion in the last chapter.

## Personality

Considerable research has been aimed at explaining the relationship between personality and performance, probably because personality appears to many to be at the center of psychological development. Despite the myriad of data, there is little agreement concerning the definition of personality or methods to measure it. Numerous cross-sectional studies have compared athletes to nonathletes, athletes of one sport to those in another, and participants to nonparticipants. However, when cross-sectional studies are eliminated in an effort to assess change, very few longitudinal studies remain to suggest personality changes as a result of physical education programs of any kind. Changes which have been reported are minimal in most instances; for example, Kenneth Tillman's study of the impact of a year of physical fitness training on the personality traits of a group of "low fit" high school boys revealed almost no shifts in personality (only clerical preference changed)[42].

One area which has received considerable attention is the potential contribution of athletic participation to "character development." Bruce Ogilvie and Thomas Tutko [28] have argued from their data on the personality traits of athletes that a "ruthless selection process operates at all levels of sport" which selects for inclusion in athletics those who already possess desirable personality traits (desirable in that they lead to success). Those individuals with "weaker" personalities are not provided with an opportunity to be transformed but instead are told to find something else in which to succeed. Jack Schendel's three-year longitudinal study of male high school athletes and nonathletes in Eugene, Oregon is perhaps even more instructive [35]. Among other things, Schendel found that nonathletes experienced more profound changes over the three-year period, especially in self-assurance, poise, and ascendency, than did athletes. Those traits related to self-perceptions such as sense of self-worth, individuality, and confidence in social interaction improved more drastically for the nonathletes. These traits also improved for the athletes, but to a more moderate extent. Part of the answer to this surprising result is found in ninth-grade comparisons of athletes and nonathletes which showed the athletes to possess a high sense of self-worth and self-acceptance at that time, thereby reducing the chance for large improvements after ninth grade. The rest of the answer may be found in the process of social maturation during the high school years; the athletes may have matured before the ninth grade whereas the nonathletes may have experienced greater maturation during the high school years. Schendel's study also pointed out the favorable personality traits of all students who were active in school affairs, and the personality trait gap between substitute athletes, who did not improve in self-acceptance, and all other subjects, including nonathletes, who did improve. This study pointedly demonstrates the danger of claiming too much for athletics in the realm of character development.

## Perceptions of Self and Body

The struggle to conceptualize personality in a way that will make it amenable to measurement resembles the confusion surrounding the measurement of self- and body-perceptions. There have been a flood of concepts—e.g., self-concept, self-esteem, body-image—but little agreement on how to measure them. Despite this state of affairs, the relationship between perceptions of self and perceptions of one's body has been repeatedly demonstrated experimentally; for example, Warren Johnson points out that a child's self-perception is "highly conditioned" by what his body can do [14].

A host of before-and-after studies have investigated self- and body-perceptions for such diverse subjects as children with physical disabilities, Little League and junior high school athletes, college students and athletes, adults, and hospitalized male psychotics. Despite the conceptual and measurement confusion, these studies for the most part show positive changes—that is, both perceptions of self and perceptions of body seem to improve in comparison to control groups as the physical education program progresses—although the reasons for such changes are not clear. Perhaps just paying attention to the subjects caused some change, or perhaps subjects reported what they felt the investigators expected from them. At any rate, physical fitness programs appear to be more successful than other kinds of physical education experiences in bringing about these kinds of changes. Although R. J. Havighurst has theorized that learning motor skills at an early age enhances self-esteem [10], the evidence from studies which focus on motor skills instruction appears to be equivocal so far, as well as confused by the number of variables in each study. For example, positive changes have been found to be related to both seventh-grade athletics and to neuromotor training for disabled children, but not to Little League.

The link between physical and intelligence factors will be mentioned briefly here because of the probable effect of intelligence changes on self-perceptions. A. H. Ismail cites evidence that physical education programs have had a positive influence on the intellectual achievement scores of both children and adolescents but not on their IQ scores [12]. However, IQ changes have been reported for mentally retarded children after experiencing a physical education program [40]. Perhaps achievement in a physical education program, especially if that program is highly valued, causes the participants to try harder on intelligence tests and to score higher on those tests which are more easily influenced by the respondent's attitude. The test results could in turn affect the individual's self-perceptions, although this is conjectural at present.

## Socially Approved Behavior

Since social approval can be an influential factor in a person's perceptions of himself and of his behavior, evidence which suggests that the development of physical abilities can lead to social approval is relevant to our discussion. This evidence is both far from complete and is largely descriptive in nature, departing from the experimental data introduced so far in this chapter. It is presented as an effort to probe the connection between physical education and social approval rather than as a definitive statement.

To substantiate the argument that the American culture highly values the subject matter of physical education, one only need pick up the sport section of any newspaper. But the issue is more complex. The value assigned to physical activity by the culture depends on sex and age of the participant, and the specific activity which he is contemplating. The young child sees a large segment of his world as play. He likely views his body and his self in almost identical ways, because how he feels about himself depends largely on how well he plays, or how he perceives himself to play. In this view, play is a central determinant of self-perception in childhood. Since play occupies so much of the child's time and energy, it may be also one avenue for acquiring the proper behavior for group approval. This cannot be clearly extracted from the literature, however, because of strong parental influences on this age group.

As the child grows older, he is socialized into his own sex role which in turn defines for him the kinds of play activities appropriate to his sex. For example, girls learn to become "little ladies." In adolescence, boys generally show interest in physical performance and competition and want to look like professional football players, while girls become increasingly interested in physical appearance and desire to look like fashion models. Girls have identified grace and coordination as definite assets, and boys have demonstrated a complex network of adolescent concerns including height, strength, physique, and sufficient achievement in both academic and athletic endeavors.

Several studies have shown a strong relationship between athletic participation and social acceptance for adolescent boys, indicating that, at least until recently, the varsity letter, particularly in certain sports, gives those who earn it prestige and popularity in the group. Robert Malina has suggested that athletics provide adolescent boys with a "rite of passage" or proving ground for manliness which would certainly enhance the role of athletics in the socialization process [23]. For girls, popularity with boys, one criterion of social status, elevates the value of physical appearance and feminine characteristics.

Just as play, sport, and exercise provide opportunities for social approval, so too do school athletics, at least in theory. In addition to the popularity or social status often associated with athletic participation, athletics also channel the energies of involved students in a socially approved direction—a direction which is reinforced by training rules reflecting the society's prescriptions for youth.

By competing against other schools, athletics also provide an "enemy" outside the group for teachers, parents, and students alike. Several causal explanations of delinquent behavior suggest that athletics may deter delinquency. In these theories, delinquency is related to weak social controls, rebellion against the school, boredom, the need to assert masculinity, association with delinquents, and being labeled as a delinquent. Athletics may be able to deter any of these sources of delinquency; it can provide strong social controls, identification with the school, something to do, masculine activities, association with nondelinquents, and labeling as an athlete. Walter Schafer examined the records of high school boys from two schools in an effort to test these theories, and found significant differences in delinquency incidence between athletes and nonathletes in the blue collar–low grade point average group [34]. However, because this study is cross-sectional in nature, it does not demonstrate conclusively that athletics change behavior. (It may be that those individuals attracted to athletics are nondelinquents from the start, that once again a selection process operates to exclude potential delinquents.) Data are not now available which will provide definitive answers to these questions.

What about adulthood? Behavioral research in physical education has only shown that neither sex in this age group is very active physically after adolescence. Therefore, we can only hypothesize about the socialization function of sport and exercise in adulthood. It appears that, for men, sports page knowledge and sport spectator activity, including hours in front of the television set during the weekend "sports marathon," function as indicators of behavior approved by the male group, even though somewhat dissapproved by the female segment in many families. Past athletic prowess also seems to serve this purpose for men —in fact, those who have not had an athletic experience of any significance sometimes create these experiences, and perhaps eventually believe that they are true, to gain approval by the group. It is not uncommon to find a bulging, balding, beer drinking TV watcher who refers to his athletic past a little too frequently. For women, exercise probably takes on added importance in the group because of the view that physical appearance increasingly depends less on "what you have" and more on "what you do." A trend toward more participation by women in exercise clubs, adult fitness programs, home exercise regimens, and jogging around the neighborhood is apparent. The participant expects to improve her physical appearance which is desired partly for social approval. All of this is merely speculative, but the hypotheses presented here could be translated into researchable problems.

## Release of Tension, Anxiety, and Aggression

One of the most frequent outcomes often associated with both sound mental health and socially approved behavior attributed to physical education is the participant's release of anxiety, aggression, and tension. The psychoanalytic school of thought views sport—both participation and spectating—as a major outlet for the aggressions and basic impulses which, if allowed full expression, would make group living untenable. Sport as an outlet reduces the effort necessary by the ego and superego to repress these impulses.

This view is seriously challenged by several generalizations drawn from research. It appears from Layman's reviews of literature [18, 19] that the expression of an impulse may generate rather than reduce the intensity of feelings of guilt and tension. Whether this occurs depends on several factors: the amount of frustration experienced by the participant who is trying to express his aggression perhaps in the face of a stronger opponent or rules of conduct which encourage sportsmanship; whether anger is present; whether the participant wins or loses; the initial personality stability of the participant; the intensity of loyalties developed by the participant in relation to the contest; the degree of emphasis on winning; and whether hostility is carried over after the activity has ended. One characteristic common to all of these factors is structured competition, suggesting that competitive and noncompetitive physical activities affect aggression, tension, and anxiety in significantly different ways. Layman suggests that dance may be particularly beneficial in this regard [18], but to move beyond speculation it is necessary to turn to studies which have experimentally investigated both competitive and noncompetitive activities. Unfortunately, such evidence is scarce.

Several studies have been conducted to test in a direct manner the hypothesis that activity releases aggression. Investigations of athletes both before and after athletic events and cross-sport comparisons including control groups show mixed results. One of the few indications of clear support for the hypothesis can be found in a recent master's thesis which focused on aggression measured by a paper-and-pencil test before and after handball matches [2]. Aggression was reduced for 23 of 32 subjects, and these reductions were not accompanied by any pattern of winning or losing. However, E. Dean Ryan's laboratory study demonstrates the complexity of this issue [33]. He had an accomplice anger some subjects and not others, all of whom participated in one of four activities including both a winning and a losing situation with the accomplice. He concluded that there was "no simple drainage of these tendencies due to physical activity" and that none of the four activities effectively reduced the general level of aggression.

## Value Transfer

Related to socially approved behavior as an outcome of the physical education experience is the socialization of participants into diffuse roles, more commonly referred to as value transfer. This concept refers to a pattern of behavior, such as being a leader or being cooperative, which is taught in one situation and then carried out in other situations. We often hear coaches claim that football teaches discipline or that sport leads to fair play in life; these are examples of value transfer. Sociologists differentiate between diffuse roles—such as democratic citizen, high achiever, and honest person—and specific roles—for example, player, coach, and referee. Because diffuse roles tend to cut across specific roles, the diffuse roles are considerably more difficult to learn. If physical educators are to influence a student's diffuse roles, sport behavior such as sportsmanship must be transferred to societal behavior.

Several writers have weighed the factors which affect the extent of value transfer in a given situation. Apparently, transfer requires specific explanations on the part of the teacher or coach relating what is happening "on the field" and what happens "in life." In other words, transfer must be taught; it does not occur automatically. In addition, transfer is more likely to occur if the situational expectations are similar in both sport and society, if the activity is voluntary such as varsity athletics as opposed to a required course, and if the participants are really involved as in the case of a first string player.

The socializing agent—that is, the teacher or coach—is at the center of several important questions. Does he have a close emotional relationship with those individuals being socialized, or is it a distant relationship? How many socializing agents are competing for attention? The physical educator's impact will not be very significant if he is only one of a number of social stimuli. Other factors—for example, a rural setting —can reduce the number of potential socializing agents, and therefore increase the impact of the central agent. What is the prestige and power of the socializing agent? In the American culture, a winning coach will have more influence than a competent physical educator. Finally, does the socializing agent demonstrate a consistent value system of his own? The often quoted hypothetical football coach who told his players: "And remember that football develops individuality, initiative, and leadership; so get in there and do exactly as I tell you" makes his unfortunate point without further elaboration.

Sheehan and Alsop's concept of educational sport [36], briefly described in the last chapter, is anchored in the proposition that values can be taught through sport and transferred to the larger society. Sheehan spells out in some detail the strategy for accomplishing this task: first, the sport must be learned; second, lectures and discussions must take place concerning the value as it operates in the sport that has been learned; third, the value must be pointed out during participation in the sport; finally, wrap-up lectures and discussions must be centered on examples of this value in the society and the means by which such a value in sport can be transferred to society. We can use cooperation in basketball to demonstrate how to transfer values. The unit should begin with basketball fundamentals and then proceed to a discussion of cooperation in basketball, stop-action examples of cooperation and failure to cooperate in basketball play (similar to stop-action examples of good and poor skills and strategies), and finally to a discussion of cooperation in society and how cooperation in basketball is related to cooperation in society. Sheehan has directed several studies which tend to substantiate his propositions (e.g., teaching cooperation using soccer, teaching positive attitudes toward carry-over activities using a required physical education course, teaching positive attitudes toward physical education using college physical education courses).

Several studies have investigated a fundamental value-oriented question that may not deal to any extent with transfer: What happens to attitudes toward sportsmanship as a result of physical education programs? The answer, from several sources, is clear, although the genesis is not: sportsmanship attitudes get worse both as children get older and as they become involved in varsity athletics. Harry Webb [44] argues that this deterioration of sportsmanship simply reflects the culture and more specifically the culture's product, urban-industrial man. Perhaps most sports programs only mirror cultural values such as competitive achievement. If so, values are being transferred in reverse: from the society into sport. This proposition is examined further in the next chapter. On the other hand, evidence of deteriorating attitudes toward sportsmanship may be a reflection of sport's influence on behavior; these attitudes may be carried from sport to society. So far the research has not identified causal factors.

Another dimension of value transfer involves the unplanned transfer of values. One study [31] suggests that soccer club involvement by immigrants insulates these individuals from the American value system. In this case, values of the American culture are less likely to be transferred to immigrants because they are involved in sport. This principle may also apply to other programs comprised primarily of immigrants. A different kind of unplanned transfer is the subject of a paper by John Phillips and Walter Schafer [29] who contend that varsity athletes tend to learn certain values from the athletic subculture which transfer to the larger society, such as deification of the educated man and disapproval of radical political activity. Values are thereby transferred from the athletic subculture to the rookie athlete's behavior in society.

## Leadership

One diffuse role which deserves special attention is leadership. Learning to lead certainly influences an individual's social-psychological growth, and physical education has given its share of lip service to this objective. It is usually argued that physical education produces leaders in at least two ways: by teaching field leadership in athletics, which transfers to society, and by developing physical ability and appearance, which serves as the basis for male and female childhood and adolescent leadership roles. Some evidence does support the contention that an important criterion for childhood and adolescent leadership positions is physical ability for boys and physical appearance for girls, but research has not yet been able to substantiate the transfer of field leadership to society. Probably the most extensive effort to prove that physical education is a force in the development of democratic leadership can be found in William Exum's doctoral dissertation, which carefully analyzes the potentialities for leadership development in a variety of physical activities [8].

## Social Mobility

Another possible social outcome of the athletic experience is improved social position, the literature of which John Loy has reviewed in considerable detail [20]. He notes that sport lore is filled with "rags to riches" stories in which athletic fame has elevated the social and economic status of such sports figures as Willie Mays, John Unitas, Bill Russell, and Bob Cousy. Even sociologists are prone to state that college athletics have improved both the social and economic positions of many players—without citing any evidence.

What are the possibilities and what evidence is available? Three mobility mechanisms for sport exist: landing a position on a professional team which carries with it a favorable social position in society; receiving an athletic scholarship to go to college which leads to educational attainment and therefore a favorable social position; and developing attitudes and behavior patterns, such as achievement, favored by the larger occupational world.

Because most of the studies concerned with social mobility are cross-sectional, the reader cannot tell how much mobility, if any, occurred in these studies. However, a few well-controlled studies have shown considerable mobility as well as greater aspirations to move up the social ladder among athletes whose socio-economic background typically restricts mobility and aspirations for social mobility in comparison to nonathletes. Athletes have fared as well or better than nonathletes in academic achievement, completion of high school, and college plans. Apparently, social mobility is sparked by organized sport, but the percentage of those affected has yet to be established. It may be that more athletes are frustrated by their failure to achieve mobility out of the ghetto through sport than those who actually succeed, but research has yet to provide answers to this question either.

## Sociometry

Sociometric studies, which involve measuring the extent of acceptance or rejection between individuals in groups, have generated the hypothesis that sport in a structured setting promotes interaction and thereby increases social acceptance. A number of investigations have been conducted over periods of several weeks in high school and college physical education classes, mostly with women as subjects. In general, these studies have reported an increase in acquaintances, reduction of isolates, increase in leaders, and improvement in social positions as the result of interaction in a physical education class. At least one study [26] has attempted to investigate the effect of manipulating social relationships in both competitive and cooperative settings on these social relationships. Although the results are not conclusive, this approach appears to be more fruitful than simply pre- and post-testing a physical education class.

In a recent study [22] four biracial groups of black and white junior high school boys were systematically observed and tested during a flag football unit to determine the effect of such interaction on various attitudes and friendship choices. Although post-tested racial attitudes were not significantly altered from pre-test scores, this kind of extended interaction did serve to weaken color as a criterion for selecting friends —that is, friendships began to form across racial groups.

## Self-Actualization

One theoretical consideration from the last chapter which has not been considered in this chapter is physical self-actualization which, if it means the actualization of one's potentialities, should include the development of physical ability. The question, then, is: Do we have evidence to support the development of physical ability in both programs and activity patterns.

The literature is replete with data supporting the notion that physical fitness development (e.g., strength, aerobic capacity) of even the low fit is well within reach. The research studies tend to examine small numbers of subjects and highly motivated, well-trained teachers—but perhaps these are key factors in devising a physical education program which works. However, Joan Nessler's review of studies which investigate the effect of remedial programs on the motor skills of poorly skilled students clearly points out the limited influence of such programs. Specific skills have been improved, but these students "remain inferior and cannot compensate for the deficiencies incurred from a dearth of practice during childhood" [27]. It is important to recognize that much of the research has concentrated on programs spanning only a few weeks or months which intervene rather late in a student's school career. Truly longitudinal studies and earlier intervention may yield more promising results. In fact, there is evidence that children as young as two years of age can improve their motor skills in a planned program [9].

If programs can be devised which will foster physical ability development, to what extent is this being accomplished in current practice? This question is difficult to answer because descriptive studies of current programs do not adequately sample all the programs in the United States. In many instances, descriptions of programs are submitted by the staff of that institution in an effort to gain recognition for an innovative program, a practice which skews the literature in the direction of innovation and change. Taking these innovative programs into account, it remains that, on a coast-to-coast basis, physical education programs tend to be characterized by crowded conditions and inadequate facilities, to be directed by tired and sometimes uninspired teachers, to be least frequent in the early years, and to be overshadowed by male interscholastic athletic programs which are often viewed as a separate entity (in contradiction to the concept of physical education programs presented in the first chapter). Whether much physical ability development takes place in programs of this nature is conjectural, but the direction that these programs frequently take suggests that "good" performers in culturally approved activities probably get at least somewhat better but that anyone who appears to be mediocre or worse will not get much exposure to good instruction and therefore will probably not improve either his motor skills or his level of fitness even if (a big "if") he continues to attend class regularly. These general comments are not meant to demean the flood of perceptual-motor programs, physical fitness programs, or other well-meaning and often effective efforts to improve physical abilities; it is simply that these kinds of programs do not typify what is currently going on across the nation but instead represent a small percentage of the whole.

Turning to patterns of physical activity, the immediate question is whether activity without instruction at any age results in physical ability development. The answer depends on a number of factors: the kind of activity—e.g., a pattern of jogging will usually lead to improved aerobic efficiency and a pattern of push-ups will lead to improved muscular endurance of certain muscle groups; the ability of the individual to observe and copy a correct performance in others; and motivational factors. The articulation of a pattern of activity with a program of instruction, such as in learning volleyball skills and strategies and then playing intramural volleyball, enhances the probability that development will occur. For children, it has been established that physical growth and development is stimulated by physical activity without instruction.

Whether patterns of physical activity hold the potential for developing physical abilities is once again only half the question; the other half is to what extent is anyone participating in anything? There is good evidence that activity levels are high for children, that they decline through adolescence, then stabilize into forty or more years of sedentary living. Although it appears that more adults are jogging, playing golf and other recreational pursuits, and joining exercise programs of one kind or another, studies by Gerald Kenyon [16] and H. J. Montoye [24] and the recent discussion by Wynn Updyke and Perry Johnson [43] show that American adults are largely a nation of spectators.

The remaining dimensions of self-actualization which have relevance for physical education are creative expression through movement and total involvement in physical performance. Evidence suggests that a number of opportunities for development of creative expression exist, particularly in dance and movement exploration. Further, these programs as well as literature describing such innovations have been growing recently, but it appears that traditional programs still easily outnumber efforts to introduce dance and movement exploration. That total involvement is a viable proposition is supported by Daryl Siedentop's statement that "recent physical education literature is replete with phenomenological descriptions" similar to the one quoted in the last chapter [37]. A discussion of phenomenology as a valid method for producing evidence reaches beyond the scope of this book; however, this approach, which in at least one of its forms utilizes highly personal descriptions of one's experience, appears to be extremely useful for investigating total involvement in physical performance as one aspect of self-actualization. It may be that total involvement is related to the release of tensions and anxieties discussed earlier to the extent that a person's worries must be left behind if he is to become totally involved. However, such involvement may not diminish the anxieties but only provide a place away from trouble for a while. Again, research has not answered these questions.

## Summary

It has been the purpose of this chapter to present evidence concerning both the propositions of the last chapter and, more broadly, the variety of claims concerning social and psychological outcomes that can result from physical education programs and patterns of activity.

Probably the major finding is that character development is a misleading, or at least confusing, term when it is used to describe social and psychological changes. A number of kinds of changes are possible, but each involves a specific concept and specific measurement techniques. Further, it appears that athletic programs do not "build character," at least to the extent that this term refers to changed personality traits. Nor is the transfer of desirable values from sport to society guaranteed according to available research.

Research also tends to dispel another common assertion, namely, that all forms of physical activity release aggression, tension, and anxiety. Again, this issue is more complex than the treatment it usually receives. In addition, doubt is even cast on the notion that most current physical education programs promote physical ability development, thereby jeopardizing at least one part of the argument that social development is an automatic concomitant value of current programs. It has been established, however, that physical ability can be developed at least to some extent in an ideal setting; it remains to devise programs which meet this objective and then to measure concomitant learnings.

The evidence, although scarce in many instances, appears to support several changes in response to physical education programs and physical activity patterns. Perceptions of both self and body have been altered by experimental programs, especially physical fitness programs, as have intellectual achievement scores, but the reasons for change are still obscure. Physical ability development probably enhances social approval, although sex and age are major factors in determining the extent of influence. However, care should be exercised in linking athletic programs to delinquency prevention and in citing physical activity as an outlet for tension and anxiety release, both of which could lead to more socially approved behavior. Values are probably transferable, both in planned and unplanned ways, but the conditions for such transfer are specific and the evidence is scanty. Athletic programs do provide an avenue for upward mobility into higher socio-economic groups, but the percentage of athletes who actually move up as the result of athletics is not known. Finally, positive changes in social relations in physical education programs have been reported based on sociometric techniques.

The influence of physical education programs and physical activity patterns on self-perceptions and, as a result, on self-esteem has not been investigated directly, but the evidence does suggest that self-perceptions can be altered by physical ability development. Although a humanistic physical education eventually requires the individual to free himself from cultural restrictions, the evidence also suggests that social approval, improved social relations, and improved socio-economic status can initially provide a base of support. According to both theory and research, interpersonal relations as a value can be taught, and the sociometry studies support the feasibility of improving interpersonal relations through sport. Physical development, creative self-expression, and total involvement as aspects of self-actualization are distinct possibilities although not substantial realities at present. Self-understanding through physical education programs has not been investigated to any extent, especially in relation to whether the integration of physical ability needs, interests, and talents into a life style is really possible as the result of guidance in a physical education program.

# References

1. AAHPER. *Values in Sport.* Washington, D.C.: AAHPER, 1962.

2. Berger, Harlan. "Court Play Can Reduce Aggressions." *Handball,* XXI (October 1971), 21.

3. Clausen, John A. "Perspectives on Childhood Socialization." In *Socialization and Society,* edited by John A. Clausen, pp. 130–81. Boston: Little, Brown and Company, 1968.

4. Coleman, James S. *Adolescents and the Schools.* New York: Basic Books, Inc., Publishers, 1965.

5. Cooper, Lowell. "Athletics, Activity and Personality: A Review of the Literature." *Research Quarterly,* XL (March 1969), 17–22.

6. Cratty, Bryant J. *Social Dimensions of Physical Activity.* Englewood Cliffs, N.J.: Prentice-Hall, Inc., 1967.

7. Dwyer, Johanna, and Mayer, Jean. "Psychological Effects of Variations in Physical Appearance During Adolescence." *Adolescence,* III (Winter 1968–69), 353–80.

8. Exum, William. "The Contributions of Physical Education Activities for the Development of Democratic Leadership Abilities." Ed.D. thesis, New York University, 1957.

9. Flinchum, Betty M., and Hanson, Margie R. "Who Says the Young Child Can't?" *JOHPER*, XLIII (June 1972), 16–19.

10. Havighurst, R.J. *Developmental Tasks and Education.* Chicago: University of Chicago Press, 1948.

11. Hellison, Donald R. "Physical Education and the Self-Attitude." *Quest*, XIII (January 1970), 41–45.

12. Ismail, A.H. "The Relationship Between Motor and Intellectual Development." In *New Perspectives of Man in Action*, edited by Roscoe C. Brown, Jr., and Bryant J. Cratty, pp. 115–29. Englewood Cliffs, N.J.: Prentice-Hall, Inc., 1969.

13. Jersild, Arthur T. *In Search of Self.* New York: Teachers College Press, 1952.

14. Johnson, Warren R. "Some Psychological Aspects of Physical Rehabilitation: Toward an Organismic Theory." *Journal of the Association for Physical and Mental Rehabilitation*, XVI (November 1962), 165–68.

15. Kenyon, Gerald S. "Sociological Considerations." *JOHPER*, XXXIX (November 1968), 31–33.

16. Kenyon, Gerald S. "The Significance of Adult Physical Activity as a Function of Age, Sex, Education, and Socio-economic Status." Paper presented at Midwest AAHPER Convention, Detroit, Michigan, April 11, 1964. Mimeographed.

17. Kistler, J.W. "Attitudes Expressed About Behavior Demonstrated in Certain Specific Situations Occurring in Sports." *Proceedings of the National College Physical Education Association for Men*, LX (December 1957), 55–59.

18. Layman, Emma McCloy. "Contributions of Exercise and Sports to Mental Health and Social Adjustment." In *Science and Medicine of Exercise and Sports*, edited by Warren R. Johnson, pp. 560–99. New York: Harper & Row, Publishers, 1960.

19. Layman, Emma McCloy. "Reaction: Aggression in Relation to Play and Sports." In *Contemporary Psychology of Sport*, edited by Gerald S. Kenyon, pp. 25–34. Chicago: Athletic Institute, 1970.

20. Loy, John W., Jr. "The Study of Sport and Social Mobility." In *Aspects of Contemporary Sport Sociology*, edited by Gerald S. Kenyon, pp. 101–19. Chicago: Athletic Institute, 1969.

21. McAfee, Robert A. "Sportsmanship Attitudes of Sixth, Seventh, and Eighth Grade Boys." *Research Quarterly*, XXVI (March 1955), 120.

22. McIntyre, Thomas D. "A Field Experimental Study of Cohesiveness, Status, and Attitude Change in Four Biracial Small Sport Groups." *Abstracts of Research Papers 1971.* Washington, D.C.: AAHPER, 1971, p. 83.

23. Malina, Robert M. "An Anthropological Perspective of Man in Action." In *New Perspectives of Man in Action*, edited by Roscoe C. Brown, Jr. and Bryant J. Cratty, pp. 147–62. Englewood Cliffs, N.J.: Prentice-Hall, Inc., 1969.

24. Montoye, H.J. *et al.* "Sports Activities of Athletes and Nonathletes in Later Life." *Physical Educator*, XVI (1959), 45–51.

25. Moore, Robert A. *Sports and Mental Health.* Springfield, Ill.: Charles C. Thomas, Publisher, 1966.

26. Nelson, Jack K., and Johnson, Barry L. "Effects of Varied Techniques in Organizing Class Competition upon Changes in Sociometric Status." *Research Quarterly,* XXXIX (October 1968), 634–39.

27. Nessler, Joan. "Motor Illiterates Go to College." *Bridging the Gap,* II (March 1972).

28. Ogilvie, Bruce C., and Tutko, Thomas A. "Sport: If You Want to Build Character, Try Something Else." *Psychology Today,* V (October 1971), pp. 61–63.

29. Phillips, John C., and Schafer, Walter E. "Subcultures in Sport: A Conceptual and Methodological Approach." University of Oregon, Eugene, n.d. Mimeographed.

30. Pollack, Jack Harrison. "Physical Education: Are Our Children Being Cheated?" *Family Health,* (September 1970), pp. 15–18.

31. Pooley, John C. "Ethnic Soccer Clubs in Milwaukee: A Study in Assimilation." *Abstracts of Research Papers 1969.* Washington, D.C.: AAHPER, 1969, p. 25.

32. Richardson, Deane E. "Ethical Conduct in Sport Situations." *Proceedings of the National College Physical Education Association for Men,* LXVI (December 1962), 98–104.

33. Ryan, E. Dean. "The Cathartic Effect of Vigorous Motor Activity on Aggressive Behavior." *Research Quarterly,* XLI (December 1970), 542–51.

34. Schafer, Walter E. "Some Social Sources and Consequences of Interscholastic Athletics: The Case of Participation and Delinquency." In *Aspects of Contemporary Sport Sociology,* edited by Gerald S. Kenyon, pp. 29–44. Chicago: Athletic Institute, 1970.

35. Schendel, Jack S. "The Psychological Characteristics of High School Athletes and Non-Participants in Athletics: A Three Year Longitudinal Study." In *Contemporary Psychology of Sport,* edited by Gerald S. Kenyon, pp. 79–96. Chicago: Athletic Institute, 1970.

36. Sheehan, Thomas J., and Alsop, William L. "Educational Sport." *JOHPER,* XLIII (May 1972), 41–45.

37. Siedentop, Daryl. *Physical Education: Introductory Analysis.* Dubuque: William C. Brown Company, Publishers, 1972.

38. Smith, Leon E. "Personality and Performance Research—New Theories and Directions Required." *Quest,* XIII (January 1970), 74–83.

39. Snyder, Eldon E. "Aspects of Socialization in Sports and Physical Education." *Quest,* XIV (Spring 1970), 1–7.

40. Stein, Julian J. "The Potential of Physical Activity for the Mentally Retarded Child." *JOHPER,* XLII (April 1971), 25–28.

41. "The New Physical Education." *JOHPER,* XLII (September 1971), 24–36.

42. Tillman, Kenneth. "Relationship Between Physical Fitness and Selected Personality Traits." *Research Quarterly,* XXXVI (December 1965), 483–89.

43. Updyke, Wynn F., and Johnson, Perry B. *Principles of Modern Physical Education, Health, and Recreation.* New York: Holt, Rinehart and Winston, Inc., 1970.

44. Webb, Harry. "Professionalization of Attitudes Toward Play." In *Aspects of Contemporary Sport Sociology,* edited by Gerald S. Kenyon, pp. 161–78. Chicago: Athletic Institute, 1969.

45. Zion, Leela C. "Body-Concept as It Relates to Self-Concept." *Research Quarterly,* XXXVI (December 1965), 490–95.

# 4

# *Physical Education and the American Culture:*
## *CONSTRAINING FORCES*

## *Introduction*

The proposition that physical education can contribute to man's psychological and social well-being is not meant to suggest that these contributions are a reality in American society. The previous chapter touched on several of the disparities between potentiality and reality in physical education. This chapter will explore the cultural and societal forces which tend to constrain physical education programs and activity patterns from contributing to humanistic goals.

The terms "culture" and "society" are not interchangeable. Culture refers to the entire heritage of a given people, i.e., the ideas, the skills, the patterns of behavior shared by members of a particular group at a given time. Society, on the other hand, refers to any group of human beings of all ages who constitute "a community of related, interdependent individuals."*

The value orientations of the American culture underlie most if not all of the constraining forces, but socializing agents or agencies are necessary in order to socialize members of the society into an awareness and acceptance of these value orientations. One of these agencies is the physical education profession: several of the major social institutions— family, school, religion, and government—also fulfill this role.

# Cultural Values

## SPORT AND THE CULTURE

A great deal of speculation has been directed at the question of whether the culture, in fact, influences patterns of sport and exercise, or whether what goes on in sport affects the culture. In which direction do values transfer? It may be that the effects are felt in both directions, but evidence supports the flow from the culture to sport and exercise patterns and programs. To begin, the abilities and creativity of a performer can only be expressed within cultural boundaries. *Sports Illustrated*'s description of Super-Hippie's Peace Pentathlon [29] is one of the few exceptions to this generalization; he was able to achieve such expression outside cultural sanctions (i.e., competing against only himself in five unique events). For the most part, however, an individual's physical abilities must conform to available activities and culturally acceptable modes of expression. Competition in a particular sport may take on different behavioral characteristics in different societies, depending on both the value attached to the sport by the culture and the culturally approved means for expression of the sport. An American Peace Corps volunteer had little success in his attempts to alter the priorities of his South American teen-age soccer team from thinking in terms of the social gathering with the opposing team after the game, to wanting to win the game.

Other societies also support the proposition that the culture influ-

*Webster's New World Dictionary.

ences both physical education programs and physical activity patterns. Because canoeing is of prime importance in the coastal culture of West New Guinea, balance forms the basis for most sports and evaluations of physical ability. Because the Hopi Indians teach cooperation and nonaggressiveness as a way of life, they learned to play basketball but not to keep score. The Timbira tribe in Brazil compete heatedly in log races, but winning or losing does not affect individual status because the event is part of religious activities. It is not unusual for the Tarahumara people in the Mexican highlands to conduct kickball races of one hundred to two hundred miles in which all contestants traverse the entire distance! The nature of their seminomadic lives explains their ability to persist in such sport. Soccer players in England, with the exception of the goal-keeper, are coached not to touch the ball with their hands even to save a goal: such an act is illegal and therefore unethical.

David Quentin Voigt's detailed and well-documented history of American baseball [61], a sport originally imported from Great Britain (baseball was not invented in America!), clearly illustrates the influence of the American culture on sport. Americans, placing more emphasis on winning than the British, could not understand much less tolerate the gentlemanly orientation of the game, and it was not long before the gentlemen were on the sidelines, often replaced by recruited players who, if it were known, were ineligible to play in many cases according to the rules of that era. The transformation of British rugby to American football also reflects a shift toward basic traits in the American culture such as the greater centrality of the individual. In American football, time is set aside for "plotting" strategy and assigning individuals specific roles in carrying out the strategy.

*CULTURAL VALUES*

A value can be defined as something of preferential interest or high priority which is abstract enough to act as a criterion for setting specific goals. It refers to the "degree of worth" of something, to the standards or social principles of an individual or society. Whether a value is considered to be dominant depends on the extensiveness of its influence, its duration, and the intensity devoted to seeking and maintaining it. Whereas a specific value may be limited to a small segment of the society, value orientation refers to a generalized pattern which characterizes the culture as a whole.

Probably the overriding value orientation in American society—one which has particular implications for physical education—is achievement and success. This value moves beyond personal excellence to competitive achievement. Americans do not simply value competition; they value success in competition. Competitive achievement is embedded deeply in the political, economic, social, and even religious systems of the culture. One has only to look at the way capitalism or political parties function to see a wide-ranging competitive survival-of-the-fittest element. Gunther Luschen argues, supporting his thesis with cross-cultural data, that sport only flourishes in achievement-oriented societies [38]. References to the value of sport in teaching competition, achievement, and aggressiveness illustrate the notion that the highly valued physical activities, at least for males, are those which are anchored securely in aggressive competitive achievement. Locker room slogans typify this view; perhaps a recent slogan makes the point: "Defeat is worse than death because you have to live with it."

Competitive achievement conflicts with a second value orientation in American society, humanitarianism, which refers to an attitude of concern and helpfulness. This conflict is often resolved by primary attention to the overriding value, achievement, and lip service to humanitarianism as seen, for example, in a comparison of typical school programs for varsity athletes (e.g., number of teams, quality of uniforms, planning sessions) with typical physical education programs for the low skilled and low fit (e.g., nonexistent in many schools). Yet when this conflict does not arise, humanitarianism emerges as a value orientation which often guides American thought and action, as for example in the many volunteer health agencies serving Americans.

The emphasis on competitive achievement appears to have taken priority over ethics in many aspects of the American culture, as opposed to other cultures. It has even been argued that the current "generation gap" is largely the result of a conflict over the priority assigned to ethics in the value system. Winning has always been important in interscholastic and intercollegiate athletics, raising the question of the extent to which the ends (winning) justify the means (playing the game). Several studies [33, 42, 52, 63] have shown that sportsmanship is not highly valued by players. One study [63] of over one thousand grade school children of five different grades revealed that the older the child, the lower he rated the importance of playing the game fairly. The girls consistently rated playing fairly higher than the boys. The most significant shift away from playing fairly for both sexes came between the sixth and eighth grades. Brian Sutton-Smith and John Roberts [56] have speculated based on cross-cultural data that games teach "trickery, deception, harassment . . . and foul play" in all cultures in which they are found, because they are "models of ways of succeeding over others."

According to their view, unethical behavior in American sport is largely the result of the nature of sport rather than the nature of American values, although it is important to keep in mind that, according to Luschen, sport only flourishes in achievement-oriented cultures.

One value orientation which is being challenged vigorously, especially by women's liberation groups, is the male-female sex role differentiation. The competitive achievement value has in the past been reserved for men who were expected to portray rugged individualism with a clear absence of self-disclosure, sensitivity toward others, and signs of emotion and pain. Women have traditionally been valued for their display of petite, dainty, and passive behavior as well as for their ability to function in child-bearing and home-making roles. Unlike men, they have been expected to show sensitivity, emotion, and pain. Physical activity in general and athletics in particular have supported these images by characterizing the male athlete as rugged, disciplined, win-oriented, courageous, aggressive—whereas the American female is not expected to grimace or sweat in sport! To the extent that these stereotypes persist, women are denied full participation in physical activity. Both the number of available activities and the number of meanings that an activity can hold for a participant are thereby restricted.

Another constraining force in our culture is the value orientation of work or busy-ness. Americans have traditionally been suspicious of leisure time; they often feel guilty if they engage in "too much" play. Bertrand Russell's admonition that "The YMCA must teach earnest young men to do nothing" [41] still stands as a humorous but reasonably accurate observation of the existing relationship between work and play in America. A related development as a result of the Puritan heritage has been the deprecation of the body which further devalued physical activities. The Puritan work ethic and mind-body dichotomy, rooted both in religious practices and in the New England colonies' fight for survival in a severe climate, have been eroded somewhat, and some have even argued that a new "fun morality" has emerged. No doubt Puritan attitudes toward play (in the New England colonies even games were work-oriented!) have been transformed somewhat, but vestiges of this orientation are still with us, impinging both on the individual's right to play and the physical educator's effort to gain support for his programs.

Some mention should be made of at least three other value orientations which have relevance for physical education: health as a value is often taken for granted, yet some societies have no translation for the term physical fitness; violence may be a value which influences the way in which sport is expressed; and science, one of the most pervasive value orientations in the American culture, may intrude into what A.R. Beisser refers to as the "last stronghold" of ritual, loyalty, communal involvement, and extension of the family—sport [4].

A passing reference should be made to the conflict between traditional and emergent values. Several, if not all, of the major orientations of the American culture are being challenged today: individualism by collectivism (e.g., communal living), competition by cooperation (e.g., deemphasis on competitive grading in schools), specific sex roles by personal recognition (e.g., "women's lib"), violence by pacifism (e.g., the peace movement), competitive achievement by ethical behavior (legislation to force politicians to disclose their financial sources), and toughness-aggressiveness by sensitivity toward self and others (e.g., the humanism movement). According to physical education teachers and coaches, the letter jacket and athletic status are no longer social symbols in many schools. The long-range impact of these challenges to traditional values on the culture and particularly on physical education will be discussed in Chapter five.

## The Physical Education Profession

### SOCIALIZATION

Socialization is most straightforwardly defined as the whole process by which an individual learns to adjust to a group by acquiring social behavior approved by that group. Each socializing agent—parent, teacher, clergyman, or peer—tends to socialize children according to his interpretation of the culture's value orientations. The physical education profession is influential in socializing individuals into physical education programs and activity patterns. By looking first at the physical educator's value system and then at the major factors responsible for this system we can gain some understanding of the extent to which the physical education profession operates as a constraining force in the development of a humanistic physical education.

### THE PHYSICAL EDUCATOR'S VALUE SYSTEM

Physical educators have historically been associated with hair cuts and dress standards for athletes, mandatory uniforms, straight lines, and showers for students, and sacrifice, dedication, and discipline as keys to success. According to Shirl Hoffman, the traditional methods of teaching physical education stress the teacher's ability to organize and oversee group practice experiences, and emphasize direct delivery of the message, neatness and order, and discipline and control. "The traditional method of teaching physical education relies little on the teacher's analytical prowess" [25]. Kenyon [32] found physical education majors at the University of Wisconsin to be more dogmatic and rigid in their thinking and to possess a more weakly formulated, traditionalistic philosophy of education than other prospective teachers. The undergraduate male major and, to a lesser extent, the female major "in many respects . . . is more like the student not preparing to teach."

A 1969 faculty opinion survey by the Carnegie Commission on Higher Education reported answers to several questions for thirty academic fields, one of which was physical education [36]. Over sixty thousand faculty members in American universities were polled, including 1208 physical educators. Physical education ranked second out of thirty fields in percentage of respondents characterizing themselves as strongly conservative, and also second in percentage characterizing themselves as moderately conservative. In response to the question "What do you think of the emergence of radical student activism in recent years?" physical educators ranked second in "disapprove with reservations" and fourth in "unreservedly disapprove." When asked about their position on Vietnam, physical educators topped all other academic fields in "defeat Communists whatever cost," while ranking third in "reduce commitment but prevent Communist takeover." Finally, physical education faculty members were second in percentage that voted for George Wallace in the 1968 election (1.4%) and second in percentage that voted for Nixon. Only agriculture consistently voted more conservatively on all of these issues.

Research on the personality traits of male coaches shows that, on the average, coaches have a much greater desire to achieve than their players do and, in general, a similar but intensified personality profile in comparison to the average competitor.

A related facet of the physical educator's value system involves his sensitivity (or lack of sensitivity) to the needs of the low skilled, the low fit, and the disabled. Arnold has suggested that the male physical educator is usually a mesomorph type who is most sensitive to the needs of students like himself [1]. Some preliminary data on those male majors at one state university who held more positive attitudes toward teaching low skilled and low fit students show a tendency for these students to be more progressive in their attitudes toward educational practices in general and less dogmatic in their thinking [24], the same characteristics which were notably lacking in Kenyon's study of physical education majors.

It is my opinion, based on numerous observations and discussions, that male physical educators, as a group, tend to hold a rather pessimistic attitude toward motor skill development, subscribing instead to the view that natural ability explains much of the wide range of performance levels. Jack Dunn, a successful high school baseball coach, has criticized the natural ability "theory" in his recent article on improving throwing in baseball [14]. This "natural ability" viewpoint is influenced by the professional coaches who serve as role models for all other coaching situations as well as by the competitive achievement value orientation which rewards success (the good athlete) rather than improvement (the improved athlete). This perspective, if it is valid, certainly acts to constrain self-actualization in relation to physical activity.

From a humanistic point of view, this information paints a pretty bleak picture. However, within the profession there have been expressions of dissatisfaction with the prevailing value system, for example, by Delbert Oberteuffer [46] and more recently by Merrill Melnick [44], but these are still distinctly minority opinions.

## FACTORS RESPONSIBLE FOR THE PHYSICAL EDUCATOR'S VALUE SYSTEM

If the typical physical educator emerges as a traditional, dogmatic person, can we hold the culture accountable for this condition? Sport is extremely popular in the culture, but its popularity is, to a large extent, anchored in the competitive achievement orientation of the American culture. Improving the human condition or being of service to mankind as a motivating force for becoming a physical educator usually takes a back seat to winning ball games. The AAHPER Committee on Career Opportunities, in a preliminary report of its work, addressed this issue:

> . . . too many of our recruits are entering the profession for the wrong reasons. Among these reasons are the desire to work almost exclusively with the highly skilled youngsters and a lack of interest in any activities other than traditional sports and games. . . .
> . . . it is probably . . . true that many prospective physical educators are attracted to this profession more out of a love of physical activity or sport and the desire to remain actively associated with these pursuits

than out of a wish to be of service to other people through the full development of individual human potential. [59]

Thus, not only cultural pressures but an emotional attachment to sport and exercise are stronger key motivators than humanistic concerns in the selection of physical education as a profession.

The competitive achievement value orientation must shoulder much of the responsibility for the physical educator's value system. The visibility associated with coaching, along with the potential for glory, are factors in the young male student's decision to become a physical educator, and both factors are associated with the competitive achievement value orientation of the American culture. Those physical education major students who are also athletes may pick up certain values from the athletic subculture. These values are perpetuated when athletes become coaches as in Ogilvie and Tutko's description:

> Most coaches believe that a truly good athlete is also, by definition, a red-blooded, clean-living, truth-telling, prepared patriot. [47].

In order to reduce the emphasis currently placed on competitive achievement and traditional approaches by physical educators, one change is clearly required: the profession must be viewed as a service whose goal is the improvement of the human condition, and criteria for a job well done must move beyond the scoreboard in athletic contests and well groomed straight lines of obedient participants in physical education.

Kenyon's finding that physical education majors have a weakly formulated educational philosophy [32] supports the observation that most physical education teachers are unclear about their educational goals. Their answers to questions of this nature often reveal that they are unable to explain why they teach what they teach or, more broadly, why physical education should be included in the curriculum. There is no doubt that many of these physical educators mean well and that they strongly feel that physical education is important; it is just that, despite all the rhetoric about objectives in professional preparation programs, they do not know why it is important.

## WOMEN PHYSICAL EDUCATORS

Most of these values and selection factors apply to both men and women in the profession. But women appear to be somewhat more academic—that is, their teaching is based a little more on current theory and research—and somewhat more concerned about helping those who need the help. Men frequently criticize women's programs for being too structured, and for including too much talk and analysis, while women usually refer to the men's physical education programs as "rolling out the ball" (all play, no instruction). Many of these differences are probably due to the role and influence of male athletic programs in comparison to their female counterparts. As women's sport becomes more organized, these differences may be reduced. Regardless, most of the foregoing characteristics, from dogmatism to scholarship, are overshadowed by the image of the "masculine" woman physical educator. This image has physical characteristics such as short hair, athletic stature and carriage, and severely tailored dress, while also possessing psychological femininity which rejects the female sex role in American society. Daniel Landers has shown, however, that prospective female physical educators differ from prospective education majors on only two of eleven psychological femininity categories: the educators are more restrained-cautious, and have stronger religious beliefs, both of which he links to degree of success in physical activity [35].

To the extent that women physical educators are perceived as being nonfeminine, this becomes yet another constraining force by discouraging at least some women from full involvement in sport, despite more organized and instructional programs. The women in sport topic is more fully explored later in this chapter.

### SUMMARY

This evaluation of the physical education profession's value system may seem unjust, because so many physical educators do not fit the model. Current literature does indicate a trend toward new ideas including humanistic concerns, yet the influence of Wood, Hetherington, Williams, Nash, and Oberteuffer in the past several decades has not appeared to alter the vast majority of tradition-encrusted programs in physical education. To a large extent, tradition and competitive achievement have shaped these programs and the aggregate value system of the profession continues to influence their direction. The development of a truly humanistic physical education seems to be constrained not only by outside forces but by the profession itself and the image it projects.

# *Social Institutions*

Any description of forces which help to shape a society's system of physical education cannot escape a consideration of social institutions —the family, education, government, religion, and the economy. A social institution is characterized by distinctive patterns of social interaction based upon certain interests and values which the participants share. How four of these social institutions affect physical education will be examined in this section.

## THE FAMILY

Much has been written about the influence of parents on their children, but few writers have shown how this influence relates to physical education. Although, generally speaking, parents are a dominant force in their children's lives, parental influence diminishes as children come into contact with both formal socializing agencies, such as school and church, and informal socializing agents, such as peers and adults other than parents. Nevertheless, the family is the earliest and most vital influence in the child's attitude toward physical activity. For boys, high achievement needs are derived from parents who set difficult goals and offer warmth and encouragement in reaching these goals. A child will generally relate emotionally to one of his parents and attempt to replicate this parent's attitudes and behavior; if the "model" parent is passive (inactive, quiet) the child will tend to behave passively into early adulthood, whereas if the parent is active the child is more apt to become dominant, aggressive, and "well-coordinated."

Parents are guided in their efforts to socialize their children—that is, to teach them social behavior which will be approved by the group —by their perceptions of the societal standards for achievement in physical development, skills, and competencies which have developed under the influence of American value orientations. Rather than strive for social adjustment for their children, today's parents generally stress competitive achievement in the form of certain behavioral expectations designed to bring the children success, at least in their parents' eyes. Achievement, of course, can be attained in numerous ways, but competition in sport certainly provides one real and very visible opportunity. The Little League and other forms of competitive sport verify this proposition. Perhaps some of this emphasis on achievement can be explained by the personality needs of the parents, but the competitive achievement value is at least partly responsible for the presence of this need.

Although family economics combined with an interest in the children determine the amount and kinds of play equipment, Cratty [12] cites evidence to suggest that disadvantaged children seem to be more creative in play (e.g., constructing play equipment) and more vigorous (without supervision or facilities) as well. It may be that lower socioeconomic status results in significantly better gross motor acceleration because these parents engage in more permissive and less exacting practices. Permissiveness does not necessarily imply passive behavior, since a parent could be both very active and very permissive. The relative effects of parental role models and parental practices on their children's physical activity patterns has yet to be determined.

### EDUCATION

Of all the social institutions, education is perhaps most closely related to structured sport and exercise programs simply because so many of these programs operate within the educational system. Education has grown in size and power in the United States in recent years. For example, between 1950 and 1960 the number of teachers increased by fifty percent, and by 1960 one out of every three Americans was somehow involved in the school system. Even viewed historically, the institution of education is probably perceived as the primary social agency for improving the social and economic conditions of Americans.

Three major purposes for the American school have evolved: (1) to indoctrinate the youth to the culture; (2) to evaluate the culture; and (3) to direct social change. The first purpose may be interpreted as indoctrination to the existing cultural values or as indoctrination to ideal social values such as freedom, democracy, and the development of human potentialities. The first purpose has probably most affected physical education by encouraging the application of existing cultural values to sport while at the same time promoting character and social development as outcomes of the sport experience. Men's sport programs have championed survival-of-the-fittest values such as competitive achievement as well as humanistic values of cooperation, sportsmanship, and human development. Meanwhile, women's sport programs, operating in the background, reflect the male dominance value orientation of the American culture.

Power in the public schools for the most part has been in the hands of middle-class businessmen and professionals who serve on school boards. These interests seem to be intent primarily on preserving the status quo, and they are probably aided in this effort by some school administrators who, although few studies are available, are frequently older and male, and business matters oriented rather than instruction oriented. Thus physical education is perpetuated as peripheral subject matter while the sacrifice, discipline, hard work, and achievement-seeking values of team sports for boys and the public relations and spectator entertainment functions of interscholastic athletics are glorified. Schools always seem to be in financial trouble, yet athletic programs for the gifted are generally well financed while, at the same time, programs for the average and below average, for girls and for grade school children founder.

## GOVERNMENT

Control over a society is exercised by the government of that society; therefore a particular government's attitudes and policies regarding physical education should profoundly affect the extent, quality, and character of physical education programs and physical activity patterns. Government attitudes and policies depend, of course, on factors including political philosophy and the underlying ecological, demographic, and sociocultural systems which, in turn, suggest certain motives for involvement in physical education. The functions that such involvement could serve include political indoctrination, national prestige, and international goodwill as well as individualizing, socializing, nationalizing, military, labor, economic, and legislative functions. The following description will move beyond the American system to cross-cultural examples in order to provide a better understanding of the variety of possible ways in which government can influence physical education.

The Soviet sport structure and national physical fitness programs exemplify one nation's use of sport and exercise for political purposes. Sport plays a major role in the Communist Party's goals, one facet of which is excellence in performance in international competition as a means to national prestige. While athletes that show promise are given every opportunity to realize their physical potentialities, the Soviet sport program is not restricted to these high level performers. Organized sport at all levels is under strict government control, and recent legislation called for an increase in participation and proficiency among the population with the intention of eventually involving almost one quarter of the people in the USSR in sport group membership. In 1961 there were 186,000 sport groups, and national championships were being held in 46 sports, six of which had more than one level of competition. In addition, the Soviet radio begins each day with morning exercises, and periodic calisthenics sessions replace the American coffee break in factories across the nation. As a final indication of the importance attached to sport and exercise, eighteen sport periodicals are published in the USSR.

The promotion of sport has not been limited to Eastern European countries. The British government finances sport for its people from the profits of a national football pool, and, in 1961, Canada passed an "Act to encourage fitness and amateur sport" which authorized the expenditure of up to five million dollars yearly to increase participation.

In the United States, government emphasis on sport and particularly physical fitness varies with the events of the times and the interests of the president. The American government has been limited in its influence by political philosophy—involving such concepts as democracy, individualism, and freedom—even when elements of this philosophy have been misconstrued in political practice. Despite these limitations, the American government has viewed physical education at various times as a means to national prestige and international goodwill as well as serving a military function. Wars seem to cause a temporary interest in fitness and sometimes in sport. Recently the government attempted to sustain this interest by forming the President's Council for Physical Fitness, an organization which has received varying degrees of support by presidents and has been criticized for its meager budget and the absence of qualified physical educators. Despite a flurry of fitness badges and clinics, the impact of the Council on the country's fitness is questionable. Aside from its questionable influence on fitness, the fitness badge program of extrinsically rewarding the best is a questionable humanistic practice. The president's personal interest in sport and exercise may also have some influence on physical education, in that he is acting as a role model. A case in point is John Kennedy who tried to set an example of both intellectual and physical activity; he remained physically active during his term in office and wrote about the need for fitness as well [31].

Sport can serve socializing functions for the government, as is illustrated by South Africa's extension of apartheid policies to sport. However, these internal policies have not contributed to international goodwill; South Africa is being more and more isolated from international sport competition both in and outside the Olympic Games. In fact, South Africa's international exposure seems to have caused New

Zealand to reevaluate and eventually to revoke their apartheid policies in sport.

Any discussion of government's influence on physical education must at least briefly consider the modern Olympic Games. Nationalism and national prestige are apparently major objectives of the Games for many countries despite the somewhat feeble attempts of the International Olympic Committee to remove politics, nationalism, and professionalism from the Games. Scorekeeping, for example, violates the spirit of the Olympic Games, which stresses individual excellence in performance, yet since 1896 the press has named a winning nation at each of the Olympic Games. After the 1952 dispute between the United States and Russia in which both countries declared themselves the winner, the International Olympic Committee issued a statement deploring the use of a point system to determine a winner. As a result, the point system of scoring declined in popularity, but counting the number of gold, silver, and bronze medals won by each nation to determine a winner still occurs. This and other similar incidents, most recently the politics so evident in the 1972 Games in Munich, suggest that nations are using the Olympic Games for other than the intended function of providing opportunities for individuals to excel in sport; instead, several nations are promoting excellence in sport to gain national prestige and to engender a spirit of nationalism among their people.

### RELIGION

Henry Steele Commager, the eminent American historian, observed that Americans curiously have ignored the application of religious teaching to their lives while at the same time attending church regularly and professing to believe vigorously [10]. Whether the institution of religion has really had a significant impact on American thought and behavior may be conjectural, but it would appear that one thick strand in the fabric of the American culture has been the Protestant tradition, an ethic which stresses conquering nature by "puritan zeal and industry" [3] and qualities of "manly courage, self-reliance, and sobriety" [62]. The Puritan heritage attached evil connotations to both play and the body. Even when the church recognized the virtues of play, its rationale was almost apologetic, as in 1895 when the Methodist Church stated: "If amusing young people helps to save them, then the work is fully and gloriously worthy of the church" [41]. The mind-body dichotomy can be traced to early Christian attitudes in which the mind and spirit were divine and pure while the body was evil. All of these characteristics indicate the negative influence that the institution of religion has had on physical education. Despite the growth of church basketball, softball leagues, and church picnics, many Americans still feel just a little guilty about playing or playing too long. Perhaps John Webb's observation of the "hang-loose" pre-game attitude of blacks in comparison to the tensions and jitters of whites does reflect an undetected Puritan influence among whites, as he has asserted [64]. On the other hand, the competitive achievement orientation of the American culture, with its implications for athletic competition, has received part of its impetus from Puritanism in the form of values such as hard work, courage, sacrifice, and discipline, all of which have found their way into locker rooms from coast to coast.

Despite a long history which reflects negative influences, Bruce Bennett has pointed out that many deeply religious men (e.g., students of theology, ministers, evangelists) were interested in physical education, including Martin Luther (physical education would keep men from sinning), Johann Bernard Basedow, Johann Friedrich Gutsmuths, Charles Beck, the founders of the Round Hill School, Edward Hitchcock, and James Naismith, the inventor of basketball [7]. Most of these names are familiar to anyone who has studied the history of physical education; they provide evidence for a paradox concerning the relationship between religion and physical education.

One religion which developed apart from the Protestant tradition focused its attention from the beginning on fitness of the body. Viewing the spirit and the body as the soul of man, Mormons have been encouraged to practice physical fitness and to play regularly while abstaining from the intake of stimulants and depressants. Mormonism was one of the leaders in building play and sport facilities and sponsoring competitive sport within the church in America. Although Catholic and Protestant churches have recently acknowledged the role of sport in the church's work and have constructed gymnasiums and organized teams, the Church of Jesus Christ of the Latter Day Saints led the way in these developments without having to combat a long history of negative attitudes toward physical education.

## Minorities

The presence of minority groups in American society constrains physical education from the achievement of its behavioral potentialities to the extent that these groups are denied full participation in physical education programs and activity patterns. Such forces as cultural values, the physical education profession, and certain social institutions may be viewed as constraining forces, because they act to inhibit the implementation of humanistic goals; minority groups form a different kind of constraining force in the sense that discriminatory practices lead to exclusion of or reduced participation for a particular segment of the population. Further, these groups may need special attention, particularly in relation to social and psychological development.

"Minority groups" refers to individuals who not only have some identifying features in common—such as physical features, language, customs, cultural patterns—but who also collectively occupy or perceive themselves as occupying a status in the society without access to power. In other words, any socially differentiated group which is not accorded the full privileges of the society or which consciously withdraws from full participation can be labeled as a minority. Since American society has historically been dominated by the white middle class male, it would appear that the minority groups in America which deserve some attention include the lower class, Blacks, Chicanos, Indians, Puerto Ricans, and women. These groups overlap: some individuals belong to more than one minority group, for example, the lower-class Black woman.

If minorities do not enjoy the full privileges extended to others in the society, there must be some reasons. Much of the blame can be attributed to the patterns of prejudice which have developed within a cultural context. Prejudice is a negative attitude consisting of stereotyped beliefs, often based on false or distorted information, toward a group. Members of the society have personality needs, such as excuses for failure and self-esteem maintenance, and a minority conveniently provides someone to be "better than" without any effort or threat. Also, intergroup conflicts within the society provide the winner with an improved competitive position; it thus becomes advantageous to oppose minority group members in these conflicts. Finally, prejudice is encouraged by cultural traditions and by man's need to develop stereotypes in his mind in order to make sense out of the real world.

The nature of prejudice and the resulting discriminatory patterns that have become part of the American culture have left their marks on the conduct of physical education. The following discussion explores the shape and extent of this influence on a representative sample of minority groups: the disadvantaged, the black athlete, and women in sport.

*THE DISADVANTAGED*

Usually, socio-economic status is determined by some combination, of occupation, education, wealth and income, and membership or non-membership in a minority group. The disadvantaged occupy the lower rungs of both the social and economic ladders in American society. These individuals comprise a large but amorphous minority in the United States, and any attempt to treat them as one group suffers from oversimplification. Nevertheless, physical education practices, as they have developed in the American culture, do have implications for the disadvantaged, so an effort will be made to describe these individuals as a distinct minority group.

The disadvantaged are found in such diverse areas as the inner city and Appalachia. By limiting this discussion to city dwellers, some notion of the characteristics of the disadvantaged can be attained. The growth of the disadvantaged population in the city has been rapid. About thirty percent of all disadvantaged children live in large Northern cities, where they constitute fifteen percent of all school age children in those cities. In New York's Manhattan, four out of every five children are either Black or Puerto Rican. The black population in such cities as New York, Detroit, and Philadelphia has either doubled or tripled since 1940. In the city, the disadvantaged carve out their own area, known variously as the slums, the ghetto, the depressed area, or, more recently, the inner city. Slums occupy about one-fifth of the nonbusiness area of major cities; they require about half of the total municipal expenditures but contribute less than ten percent of the total revenue. Education in these areas has suffered because expenditure per pupil is less than half than that which is allotted in the suburbs and because the faculty-pupil ratio is far higher than the suburban ratio, although there have been recent efforts to rectify this imbalance. In addition, the inner city is characterized by a higher average number of children and a higher rate of broken homes.

There is some disagreement among researchers concerning the effect of socio-economic status on motivation and the learning process. For example, several studies have investigated whether being disadvantaged causes a tendency toward low self-perception, but the studies' results conflict. Inner-city children are usually depicted as possessing a depressed language function, poor auditory discrimination, poor time orientation, a tendency to ignore difficult problems with a "so what?" attitude, and a preoccupation with beauty and fame rather than moral and intellectual qualities. However, the Baratz study represents an opposing view by suggesting that many of these characteristics are middle-class interpretations which view inner-city behavior as pathological rather than as culturally different [2].

No matter which view one takes, inner-city behavior differs from the mainstream of American cultural values. Since physical education is a nonverbal mode of communication which can fulfill the urge for physical testing and for play, it possesses a unique entry into the world of the inner-city child and may be able to bridge the gap between this child's behavior patterns and the school's expectations. In addition, many of the potential outcomes of the physical education experience—improved self-perception, value transfer, and social mobility into a more favorable socio-economic status—have special relevance for the disadvantaged.

If it is true that the inner-city disadvantaged form a minority group with differentiating characteristics, and that physical education may hold certain unique potentialities for inner-city youth, what is being done to realize these potentialities? Unfortunately, the evidence is scarce. The physical education literature does reflect an upswing of interest in the inner city, but whether the conduct of physical education is responding to these needs is an unanswered question. Here and there special programs are being tried. For example, the Sports Unlimited program in Los Angeles represents an organized effort to tie competitive sport to academic achievement by organizing teams whose scores are based on both their win–loss record in sport and their academic progress. Both the utilization of major sports figures and movement exploration have also been attempted in inner-city physical education programs. It can be speculated that the traditional views of many physical educators probably make meeting the needs of the disadvantaged more difficult, if only because inner-city behavior and values fall outside the tightly organized value system of the profession.

Patterns of physical activity for the disadvantaged have historically been restricted both for economic reasons and because of discriminatory practices; such activities as golf, tennis, and swimming have been out of the reach of many Americans. A study of Black participation in public recreation and recreational administrative practices in New York City and its surrounding communities revealed considerable segregation and discrimination including poor facilities for the Blacks, few special programs in disadvantaged areas, little effort to foster integration, and distinctive patterns of sport involvement, for example, boxing, in disadvantaged neighborhoods [34].

John Loy and Joseph McElvogue have proposed that discrimination in activities involving both whites and Blacks is a function of the extent of interracial interaction during performance, the degree of separation of performance from skill in interpersonal relations, and the extent to which an individual's success depends upon his own performance rather than reliance on others [37].

## THE BLACK ATHLETE

Blacks form a large segment of the disadvantaged population in many cities, but the black athlete deserves special attention for the impact he has had on sport. In a period of rapid change in civil rights legislation, ranging from education to housing, the black athlete has begun to challenge the role sport plays in his development. Athletics have always been viewed as a way out of the ghetto, but recently sport has been on the receiving end of loud criticism and rebellious action by Blacks.

Whether sport has been "good to the Negro" rather than simply mirroring the discriminatory practices of the culture is still a debated issue. It has been argued that sport is worse than the larger society because it embraces the same discriminatory patterns while claiming to do better. The list of discriminatory practices attributed to the white athletic establishment has grown in proportion to the freedom that Blacks have felt in expressing their views. Items on this list include the stacking of black players at one position, dating restrictions aimed at eliminating contact with white girls, differential treatment in the care of injuries, prejudiced game officials in black-white contests, and inadequate facilities and scheduling problems at black schools. It does not matter whether these practices are entirely real or partially distorted; they motivate Blacks and some whites to increasingly sharp criticism of the athletic establishment as well as to protests, boycotts, and the like.

At the same time there is a growing black subculture which has as its goal the development of pride in black dress, language, and other cultural characteristics. These characteristics often run counter to the value systems and rules of coaches. Meanwhile, a whole host of black role models who are disenchanted with the "major" culture have surfaced, including such renowned athletes as Bill Russell and Tommie Smith.

All of this—the complaints concerning discriminatory practices, the emerging black subculture, and new role models—can be traced to civil rights legislation which loosened discriminatory practices that had been firmly entrenched in the American culture and to the continuing rejection of Blacks by whites at all levels of society despite formal desegregation. If the revolutionary J-curve proposed by James Davies [13] is applicable to the Blacks, it would explain the revolutionary behavior of the black athlete. This theory suggests that revolution does not occur when a particular segment of society is downtrodden, but instead when conditions begin to improve but do not improve quickly enough to suit those who were oppressed.

All of these factors affect the black athlete's view of what is happening to him in athletics. Discriminatory practices are pointed out on and off the field. Role models who advocate change include star athletes. The black subculture is challenged by some coaches who insist on enforcing rules which conflict with expectations of this subculture, causing friction or an identity crisis for the young black athlete who is trying to relate to two different sets of standards. Confrontations, protests, and boycotts result which further perplex and frustrate the white athletic establishment. Establishment reactions vary, from recruiting fewer Blacks on one hand to attempts to hire more black coaches and athletic administrators on the other.

## WOMEN IN SPORT

If it were not for the Women's Liberation Movement, labeling women as a minority group even though they outnumber the men might seem a bit humorous. Women's protest groups are being taken more seriously in a period of American history where protesting has become rather commonplace. There is little question that women fit our definition of minority group, because they belong, by reason of sex alone, to a socially differentiated group which has not been accorded the full privileges of American society. It is not the purpose of this discussion to chronicle the history of women's rights, but to focus on the extent to which and ways in which women have been treated as a minority group in sport.

The sex role of the American female has traditionally been confined primarily to that of help-mate for the American male, with child-bearing and home-making as the major criteria for fulfillment. Such occupations as nursing and elementary school teaching which do not appear to be too widely divergent from these help-mate roles have also been socially acceptable. The American woman is expected to project a feminine image at all times, to play the appropriate sex role with all the passive, dainty, and petite mannerisms she can muster. Girls begin to play their sex role in play at an early age, not only by choosing different forms of play but also by displaying different attitudes toward competition and success than boys display. For example, Malina [39] points out that girls are less able than boys to differentiate among styles of success; instead they only distinguish between good fortune and failure. Adolescent girls seem to be primarily interested in their physical appearance whereas boys aspire to excellence in physical performance, although adolescent girls have identified grace and coordination as assets in the development of a positive self-perception. Declining fitness trends have been reported for girls aged thirteen to fifteen (whereas fitness is generally thought to improve until at least the late teens), probably because at this age girls become aware that it is not feminine to be strong and fit.

These cultural expectations for women have reduced full participation in competitive sport. Certain physical activities have been more acceptable in the culture than others. For example, those activities which accentuate grace and beauty are more likely to meet with approval than those activities which are perceived to involve sweating and grimacing. If direct contact with opponents can be avoided, as in net games, and if a light implement and object are used in the activity, as in badminton and tennis, females will have more chance of retaining their femininity in the eyes of onlookers. Research has tended to support these generalizations by demonstrating that such activities as swimming, tennis, and gymnastics lead in popularity with women, while team sports, particularly basketball and softball, are least popular. In one study, those who participated in individual sports stated that these sports enhanced their femininity and dating appeal, whereas team sport participants were unsure of the contributions of sport to their femininity and tended to participate despite negative feedback [40].

Females have tried to counteract the risk of their femininity in track and field as well as other sports by adopting bouffant hairsprayed hairdos and ruffled, figure-flattering uniforms. However, it may be that there are three distinct groups of woman athletes: those who are concerned about their femininity, those whose femininity is not threatened, and those who don't care. The latter group provides evidence for the stereotype of the "girl jock."

Fortunately for the competitive-minded woman, there are signs of a significant shift in thinking about the female in American society. In addition to the variety of causes popularized by the Women's Liberation Movement, such social institutions as marriage and the family are being redefined. Marriage is increasingly seen as a companionship between husband and wife, and the working wife, mother or not, is gaining more and more acceptance. The movement has served to reduce the cultural distinctions between man and woman in style, occupation, and behavior in general. Sport, too, is slowly widening its opportunities for women, and, although women still struggle for their share of the facilities, the number of female programs and participants is on the rise. This does not mean that men have loosened their protection of the masculine image in sport. To the contrary, some of the "lethal" characteristics of the American male (primarily sex role characteristics such as failure to show pain and sensitivity) described by Sidney Jourard [30] have found their last stronghold in sport, but men seem to be gradually realizing that playing field hockey does not deprive a woman of her femininity any more than staying at home to make curtains makes her feminine. If the Liberation Movement catches on in physical education, and the recent article by Virginia Jinks in *JOHPER* indicates that it is beginning to [27], the magnitude of the ensuing change cannot be predicted.

# References

1. Arnold, Peter. *Education, Physical Education, and Personality Development.* New York: Atherton Press, Inc., 1968.
2. Baratz, Stephen S., and Baratz, Joan C. "Early Childhood Intervention: The Social Science Base of Institutional Racism." *Harvard Educational Review,* XL (February 1970), 29–50.
3. Barrett, William. *Irrational Man: A Study in Existential Philosophy.* Garden City, N.Y.: Doubleday & Company, Inc., 1962.
4. Beisser, A. R. *The Madness in Sport.* New York: Appleton-Century-Crofts, 1967.
5. Bennett, Bruce L. "Critical Incidents and Courageous People in the Integration of Sports." *JOHPER,* XLII (April 1971), 83–85.
6. Bennett, Bruce L. "Religion and Physical Education." *Physical Educator,* XIX (October 1962), 83–86.
∨ 7. Bennett, Bruce L. "The Curious Relationship Between Religion and Physical Education." *JOHPER,* XLI (September 1970), 69–71.
8. Bronowski, J. "Protest—Past and Present." *The American Scholar,* XXXVIII (Autumn 1969), 535–46.
9. Cavan, Ruth Shonie. *The American Family.* New York: Thomas Y. Crowell Company, 1963.
10. Commager, Henry Steele. *The American Mind: An Interpretation of American Thought and Character since the 1800's.* New Haven: Yale University Press, 1950.
11. Corwin, Ronald G. *A Sociology of Education: Emerging Patterns of Class, Status, and Power in the Public Schools.* New York: Appleton-Century-Crofts, 1965.

12. Cratty, Bryant J. *Social Dimensions of Physical Activity.* Englewood Cliffs, N.J.: Prentice-Hall, Inc., 1967.
13. Davies, James C. "Toward a Theory of Revolution." *American Sociological Review,* XXVII (February 1962), 5–19.
14. Dunn, Jack. "Throwing—The Key to Defensive Baseball." *Athletic Journal,* LII (January 1972), 48ff.
15. Edwards, Harry. *The Revolt of the Black Athlete.* New York: The Free Press, 1970.
16. Fairs, John R. "The Athletics–Physical Education Dichotomy: The Genesis of the Intercollegiate Athletic Movement." University of Western Ontario, London, Ontario, n.d. Mimeographed.
17. Gerber, Ellen W. "The Changing Female Image: A Brief Commentary on Sport Competition for Women." *JOHPER,* XLII (October 1971), 59–61.
18. Gerth, Hans, and Mills, C. Wright. *Character and Social Structure: The Psychology of Social Institutions.* New York: Harcourt Brace Jovanovich, Inc., 1953.
19. Goff, Regina M. "Some Educational Implications of the Influence of Rejection on Aspirations Levels of Minority Group Children." *Journal of Experimental Education,* XXIII (December 1954), 179–83.
20. Gould, Julius, and Kolb, William L. *A Dictionary of the Social Sciences.* New York: The Free Press, 1964.
21. Grambs, Jean D. "The Self-Concept: Basis for Re-education of Negro Youth." In *Negro Self-Concept,* report of a conference sponsored by the Lincoln Filene Center for Citizenship and Public Affairs, pp. 11–34. New York: McGraw-Hill Book Company, 1965.
22. Harris, Dorothy V. "The Sportswoman in Our Society." In *DGWS Research Reports: Women in Sports,* edited by Dorothy V. Harris, pp. 1–4. Washington, D.C.: AAHPER, 1971.
23. Havighurst, Robert J. "Who Are the Socially Disadvantaged?" In *Education and Social Crisis,* edited by Everett T. Keach, Jr., et al., pp. 23–30. New York: John Wiley & Sons, Inc., 1967.
24. Hellison, Donald R. "Attitudes Toward Teaching Low Skilled and Low Fit Students Among Physical Education Majors." *Abstracts of Research Papers 1971,* p. 34. Washington, D.C.: AAHPER, 1971.
25. Hoffman, Shirl James. "Traditional Methodology: Prospects for Change." *Quest,* XV (January 1971), 51–57.
26. Inkeles, Alex. "Society, Social Structure, and Child Socialization." In *Socialization and Society,* edited by John A. Clausen, pp. 73–129. Boston: Little, Brown and Company, 1968.
27. Jinks, Virginia Nill. "Dance and Sexism." *JOHPER,* XLII (March 1971), 83–85.

28. Johns, Glenn. "The President's Council Today: A Study in Futility." *Fitness for Living,* IV (March–April 1970), 90–96.

29. Jones, R.F. "The World's First Peace Pentathlon." *Sports Illustrated,* XXXII (May 11, 1970), 50–58.

30. Jourard, Sidney M. *The Transparent Self: Self-Disclosure and Well-Being.* New York: Van Nostrand Reinhold Company, 1964.

31. Kennedy, John F. "The Soft American." *Sports Illustrated,* XIII (December 26, 1960), 15–17.

32. Kenyon, Gerald S. "Certain Psychological and Cultural Characteristics Unique to Prospective Teachers of Physical Education." *Research Quarterly,* XXXVI (March 1965), 105–12.

33. Kistler, J.W. "Attitudes Expressed about Behavior Demonstrated in Certain Specific Situations Occurring in Sports." *Proceedings of the National College Physical Education Association for Men,* LX (December 1957), 55–59.

34. Kraus, Richard G. *Public Recreation and the Negro: A Study of Participation and Administrative Practices.* New York: Center for Urban Education, 1968.

35. Landers, Daniel M. "Psychological Femininity and the Prospective Female Physical Educator." *Research Quarterly,* XLI (May 1970), 164–70.

36. Lipset, Seymour Martin; Trow, Martin A.; and Ladd, Everett C. "Faculty Opinion Survey." Carnegie Commission on Higher Education, n.d. Printed.

37. Loy, John W., and McElvogue, Joseph F. "Racial Integration in American Sport." Paper presented at the International Seminar on the Sociology of Sport, Macolin, Switzerland, September, 1969. Mimeographed.

38. Luschen, Gunther. "The Interdependence of Sport and Culture." *International Review of Sport Sociology,* II (1967), 127–41.

39. Malina, Robert M. "An Anthropological Perspective of Man in Action." In *New Perspectives of Man in Action,* edited by Roscoe C. Brown and Bryant J. Cratty, pp. 147–62. Englewood Cliffs, N.J.: Prentice-Hall, Inc., 1969.

40. Malumphy, Theresa M. "Athletics and Competition for Girls and Women." In *DGWS Research Reports: Women in Sports,* edited by Dorothy V. Harris, pp. 15–20. Washington, D.C.: AAHPER, 1971.

41. Martindale, Don. *American Society.* Princeton, N.J.: Van Nostrand Reinhold Company, 1960.

42. McAfee, Robert A. "Sportsmanship Attitudes of Sixth, Seventh, and Eighth Grade Boys." *Research Quarterly,* XXVI (March 1955), 120.

43. McIntosh, P.C. *Sport in Society.* London: Watts, 1963.

44. Melnick, Merrill J. "Footballs and Flower Power." *JOHPER,* XL (October 1969), 32–33.

45. Morton, Henry W. *Soviet Sport.* New York: P.F. Collier, Inc., 1963.

46. Oberteuffer, Delbert. *Man in Function . . . Man in Total.* Columbus: Spahr and Glenn, 1966.

47. Ogilvie, Bruce C., and Tutko, Thomas A. "Sport: If You Want to Build Character, Try Something Else." *Psychology Today,* V (October 1971), pp. 61–63.

48. Olsen, Jack. *The Black Athlete: A Shameful Story.* New York: Time-Life Books, 1968.

49. Phillips, John C., and Schafer, Walter E. "Subcultures in Sport: A Conceptual and Methodological Approach." University of Oregon, Eugene, n.d. Mimeographed.

50. Phillips, Madge. "Women in Sport: The Impact of Society." In *DGWS Research Reports: Women in Sports,* edited by Dorothy V. Harris, pp. 5–14. Washington, D.C.: AAHPER, 1971.

51. Purkey, William. *Self Concept and School Achievement.* Englewood Cliffs, N.J.: Prentice-Hall, Inc., 1970.

52. Richardson, Deane E. "Ethical Conduct in Sport Situations." *Proceedings of the National College Physical Education Association for Men,* LXVI (December 1962), 98–104.

53. Riesman, David, and Denney, Reuel. "Football in America: A Study in Cultural Diffusion." In *Sport, Culture, and Society,* edited by John W. Loy, Jr., and Gerald S. Kenyon, pp. 306–19. New York: The Macmillan Company, 1969.

54. Semotiuk, Darwin M. "The Development of Theoretical Framework for Analyzing the Role of National Government Involvement in Sport and Physical Education and Its Application to Canada." Unpublished Ph.D. dissertation, The Ohio State University, Columbus, 1970.

55. Sexton, Patricia Coys. *The American School: A Sociological Analysis.* Englewood Cliffs, N.J.: Prentice-Hall, Inc., 1967.

56. Sutton-Smith, Brian, and Roberts, John M. "The Cross-Cultural and Psychological Study of Games." In *The Cross-Cultural Analysis of Sport and Games,* edited by Gunther Luschen, pp. 100–108. Champaign: Stipes, 1970.

57. Thompson, Richard. *Race and Sport.* London: Oxford University Press, 1964.

58. Tottossy, Miklos, and Wettan, Richard. "The Cold War and the Olympic Games." *Proceedings of the National College Physical Education Association for Men,* LXXIV (December 1970), 217–22.

59. Updyke, Wynn F. "A Backward Glance at Priorities." *JOHPER,* XLII (March 1971), 79.

60. Uys, Stanley. " 'No' to Arthur Ashe." *New Republic,* CLXII (February 14, 1970), pp. 17–18.

61. Voigt, David Quentin. *American Baseball: From Gentleman's Sport to the Commissioner's System.* Norman: University of Oklahoma Press, 1966.

62. Waller, George M., ed. *Puritanism in Early America.* Boston: D. C. Heath & Company, 1950.

63. Webb, Harry. "Professionalization of Attitudes toward Play." In *Aspects of Contemporary Sport Sociology,* edited by Gerald S. Kenyon pp. 161–78. Chicago: Athletic Institute, 1969.

64. Webb, John. Lecture on the body in the American culture to sport sociology class, San Fernando Valley State College, Northridge, California, March 1971. Transcription of tape recording.

65. "What Has Recent Research Said About Teaching the Disadvantaged?" *Today's Education,* LIX (January 1970), 14.

66. Williams, Robin M. *American Society: A Sociological Interpretation.* New York: Alfred A. Knopf, Inc., 1951.

67. Wyrick, Waneen. "How Sex Differences Affect Research in Physical Education," edited by Dorothy V. Harris. *DGWS Research Reports: Women in Sports,* pp. 21–30. Washington, D.C.: AAHPER, 1971.

68. Young, A. S. *Negro Firsts in Sports.* Chicago: Johnson Publishing Co., 1963.

# 5

# Prospects for Change

## Humanizing Physical Education

It is time to review the major themes presented so far as a precursor to a discussion of the prospects for implementing this humanistic approach to physical education. A truly humanistic physical education embraces both formal programs and the physical activities that people typically engage in (i.e., activity patterns), and has a number of specific sequential goals, all of which are subsumed under the objective of moving each individual toward social and emotional well-being. The first goal involves elevating self-perceptions of one's physical ability to the point that self-esteem is improved, at least in relation to physical ability. The second goal is self-actualization in those dimensions which can be influenced by physical education experiences, namely physical development, creative self-expression, and the feelings and meanings associated with total involvement in a physical activity. The third goal is self-understanding, the process of introspection whereby one's physical abilities, needs, and interests are analyzed and eventually integrated into a meaningful life style. The fourth goal involves the improvement of interpersonal relations both in and outside physical education, with specific reference to cooperation and sensitivity toward others.

Whether these goals are within reach has been the subject of considerable speculation, rational thinking, and some research. The results of these efforts tend to explode some of the myths surrounding the physical education–behavioral development relationship, but humanistic goals for the profession are not jeopardized in the process. In fact, although there are wide gaps in the information currently available, several of these goals appear to be distinct possibilities. Support for related outcomes—such as social approval, improved social relations, and social mobility through physical education—can also be found.

The probability that these humanistic goals are within reach by no means guarantees their achievement, because American society has been constrained from adopting a humanistic approach to physical education by several forces. Underlying most, if not all, of these influences are certain cultural value orientations, notably competitive achievement, the male-female sex role differentiation, the absence of standards for ethical behavior, and the Puritan legacy of work and deprecation of the body. Members of the society are socialized into the physical education experience both by the physical education profession, which shares a value system based on tradition and competitive achievement and projects an image for the most part incompatible with the humanistic approach, and by parents, who tend to be guided by the dominant value orientations of the culture. The institution of education also acts as a constraining force by adhering to a narrow traditional view of the purpose of physical education in the schools. To a lesser extent, at least two other social institutions have also performed a constraining function: religion, by its support of Puritan attitudes toward work and the body, and the Federal government, by its failure to influence physical education programs and patterns in a humanistic direction. The entrenchment of discriminatory practices in the society has constrained physical education from the full realization of its potentialities for minority groups.

Daryl Siedentop has recently presented his own approach to physical education as well as a survey of the past and current state of affairs in physical education [25]. Siedentop's major concern seems to be that the humanistic approach, along with other "education through the physical" endeavors, encourages:

> an instrumental way of looking at education. A sometimes nebulous end is invented which the activities of education are supposed to lead toward; this being required because it has been assumed that education must be justified by reference to an aim which is extrinsic to it. This, it seems to me, has been one of the weaknesses of the education-through-the-physical viewpoint which attempts to justify physical education by reference to fitness and social development and, in doing so, promotes a utilitarian approach to the activities of physical education. The danger of this is that it risks losing the inherent meaning and significance of the activity. . . . It should be obvious by now that the author is convinced that the activities of physical education are self-justifying; that learning to play badminton or handball skillfully is worthwhile and sufficient cause for their inclusion in a school curriculum.

Siedentop is also concerned about what self-actualization or becoming a fully functioning person really means, and whether it can be translated into a realistic objective of physical education. Despite these doubts, he admits that the intrinsic meaning obtainable from play experiences resembles both Maslow's "peak experience" and Rogers' fully functioning person.

It is not the intention of this text to disdain or reject the intrinsic objectives of the physical education experience. To the contrary, these have been incorporated in the discussion of self-actualization. But the humanistic approach described here is only one way of looking at physical education. It appears to be important as a vehicle for social and emotional well-being, but being a vehicle is certainly not physical education's only function and perhaps not even its major function. Whether physical education will be allowed to function in a humanistic manner depends on the capacity of the current system for change.

## Mechanisms for Change

Chapter one called attention to the emergence of social and emotional well-being as an increasingly popular objective in physical education after the turn of the century. After several decades of promoting various "education-through-the-physical" views we have accomplished considerable lip service to such goals without altering the conduct of physical education. Therefore, the major question which must be addressed is: If Hetherington, Williams, Oberteuffer, and others could not change the system, how can the humanistic approach presented here expect to fare better?

To answer this question it is necessary to consider two different sets of factors: (1) the mechanisms for change that have always existed, and (2) the expanding capacity for change as the result of recent developments.

Sociologist Wilbert Moore has referred to social change as a subject which has not been studied seriously until recently [17]. Many distinguished scholars, including Pitirim Sorokin and A. L. Kroeber, have argued the case for cultural determinism—i.e., that man is similar to a blank tablet which is written upon by the culture, that the culture imprints itself on man, that man is the carrier of the culture. This view leaves little room for a concept of change which takes into account man's freedom to reflect upon his culture:

> Determinism is the doctrine that causal law prevails throughout nature and that no causes operate independently of natural law. Determinism involves belief in a totality or system of interrelations such that no thing is capable of acting independently of another. In a deterministic order of nature there can be no free cause and no real freedom of choice. [1]

Anthropologist and philosopher David Bidney [1] has opposed cultural determinism by arguing that man receives direction from his past, including both history and culture, but that he possesses the ability to reflect on his own behavior—to treat his own behavior as the object rather than the subject of his action—and to modify his behavior in line with self-reflection. Cultures can either repress or encourage this process, but, according to Bidney, they cannot eradicate this capability:

> As against this sociocultural, historical determinism, I find myself in agreement with those who take human freedom seriously and reckon with human decision as an effective, historical cause. Man's knowledge of history is itself a factor in his present decisions and may enable him to reverse the trends of the past and to choose new goals for future achievement. [1]

One of the major tenets of humanistic psychology is that individuals must develop a "selective detachment" from their culture in order to avoid mirroring the values of society and thereby inhibiting individual development. This point of view assumes what Bidney has argued: that man possesses the capability for self-reflection within a given culture. Certain conditions are necessary in order to facilitate cultural detachment: the ability to clearly and accurately differentiate the self from the culture, the ability to objectively perceive the culture and to evaluate its elements, possession of a higher valuation of the self than of the cultural prescriptions for behavior, and possession of interests, perceptions, identifications, and activities which extend beyond but which do not destroy identification with the culture. If these conditions can be achieved, the individual should be able to operate at least somewhat independently of the culture, for example by evaluating and then accepting or rejecting cultural value orientations.

In addition to man's capability for self-culture reflection, a number of mechanisms enable change to occur at the societal or cultural level. Perhaps the first of these is flexibility. The number of flexibilities and fluctuations in a given system provides the possibility and probability for change by establishing conditions conducive to change. American society is now undergoing considerable fluctuation and showing increased flexibility, which we shall discuss in detail later. A second mechanism for change involves the view of society as a loosely interdependent system of social action wherein change in any one aspect of the system may cause changes in other aspects of the system. Thus, war or Sputnik or an increase in the incidence of cardiovascular disease may spread throughout the system and influence the direction of physical education as well as other processes and institutions. Another mechanism for change is acculturation, the transfer of social or cultural elements across cultures. This mechanism opens the door to the adoption of, for example, British ideas such as the adult sport club and multi-level athletic competition. However, several factors influence the acculturation process: the simplicity of the element being introduced, the consistency of the element being introduced with existing cultural value orientations, the prestige of the other culture or of the "bearers" of the element, and the extent to which change is a part of the receiving culture. A fourth mechanism for change is the social movement, a group which desires change of some kind or wants to resist a particular change and which develops its own organization, rules and tradition, and stability and continuity in time. Two historical examples of social movements are the women's rights movement and the temperance movement. Many social movements are absorbed into the existing social institutions as the change they have advocated is adopted. Finally, the most extreme form of social change is revolution which, in its true sense, involves a complete change not only in the structure of government but also in legal codes and norms relating to other major social functions. Revolutions consist of a number of stages, the last of which often involves a return to some of the major structural features of pre-revolution society.

Since the institution of education houses the vast majority of physical education programs, those mechanisms for change which are specific to schools should be reviewed. Instead of indications of change, however, research has produced a long list of mechanisms for preserving the status quo, including the absence of valid research findings, standardization caused by the high mobility rates of both teachers and students, the lack of an economic incentive to adopt changes, lay control of the schools, ideological beliefs (e.g., teaching cannot be effectively measured), emphasis on current operations and maintenance to the exclusion of research and development, deeply established patterns of interaction and subsystems within the school which resist change, the absence of change agents to promote new ideas, community indifference and reticence, and educational bureaucracy coupled with the "rut" of experience. Despite this dreary, long-winded account of the difficulties inherent in educational change, certain change factors have been identified: cultural values such as democracy, progress, equality, and the importance of education; events such as the Cold War, growth in the knowledge industry, and advances in the behavioral sciences; the general climate for change set by numerous changes in the culture; and careful planning concerning the introduction and use of a particular innovation.

D. B. Van Dalen has argued that there are basically four producers of change in either state or local physical education programs: leadership in the profession, government legislation, cultural forces such as war, and research activity which filters down to the program level [28]. The first two of these have earlier been identified as acting presently as constraining forces. Cultural forces which affect other aspects of the society have already been described as one mechanism for change. The applied research question, raised briefly in Chapter one, has yet to be developed.

The system of physical education in the United States—including infrequent adult participation, emphasis on athletic programs in the schools, and inadequate programs for women—has managed to resist change despite efforts both within and outside the system. Yet the capacity for change exists in the form of man's capability for self-reflection in relation to cultural directives as well as a number of available mechanisms for social change. Something more is apparently needed; perhaps recent developments contain seeds for the expansion of the American society's capacity for change.

## Signs of Change

### EMERGENT VALUES

In Chapter four, emergent value orientations in the American culture were contrasted to traditional values, which were described in some detail. As Bob Dylan pointed out in one of his songs, "The times they are a-changin'." It is not just that we are in an age of protest; as J. Bronowski has noted, "Progress by dissent . . . is characteristic of human societies." [2] What American society is currently experiencing is a transformation of fundamental cultural value orientations. A loose coalition of American youth and older intellectuals are, in various ways and to varying degrees, challenging competitive achievement, questionable ethical behavior, traditional male and female sex roles, the body deprecation and work morality, and violence as guidelines for the socialization process. There is an urgent desire to redefine the criteria for interpersonal relations so that such qualities as love, peace, cooperation, sensitivity toward others, and freedom of choice to work and play as one sees fit replace the traditional value orientations and raise the priority that humanitarianism has received as a traditional value.

### THE GROWTH OF HUMANISM

Partly responding to the need for change and partly leading the movement for change, humanistic psychology has emerged as an alternative to Freudian and behaviorist schools of psychological thought. Its major concern has been to encourage people to fully experience life by using their unique talents and abilities and by understanding and expressing their feelings about themselves and others. One result has been a meteoric rise in the number of encounter groups, sensitivity sessions, growth centers, human potentiality workshops, and the like, coupled with increasing reference to the development of a "counter-culture" which clearly represents an alternative to traditional cultural values. Although this movement has taken several forms including both conservative and liberal approaches, its presence is an important indicator of changing cultural values.

The humanistic movement has recently expanded its influence beyond the borders of psychological thought and its application to individual life styles to touch both sociology and education. Humanistic sociology has a primary commitment to a concern for man and has as its central task:

> to ask which institution and social arrangements, supported by which values and norms, promote the capacity and ability of groups and individuals to make free and responsible choices in the light of their needs to grow, to explore new possibilities, and to do more than simply survive. [7]

Although there is little agreement concerning the extent of influence of the humanistic movement in sociology, sociology is clearly witnessing the rapid growth of a variety of theoretical frameworks including humanistic sociology.

The field of education has also felt the intrusion of humanism as indicated by a wave of recent books focusing both on the relationship between schools and self-concept and, even more to the point, on humanism in education. All these works direct attention to the learner's needs, abilities, interests, and feelings and relate the educational process to a concern for human well-being. For example, Fantini and Weinstein, in their book *Toward Humanistic Education: A Curriculum of Affect*, describe in detail a teaching-learning model which places primary importance on how the learner feels—about himself, about others, about the subject matter [6]; Carl Weinberg's *Humanistic Foundations of Education* presents a variety of humanistic perspectives toward different aspects of education [29]. Once again a trend is not clear, but these examples indicate a shift in values in education.

### CHANGE IN PHYSICAL EDUCATION

Both the physical education profession and the world of sport are bending to the winds of progressive thought. In physical education, scholarship has taken a firm hold, and everything from traditional approaches to physical training to locker room slogans are under scrutiny. The newer textbooks in the field demonstrate that physical education has arrived in academic circles, not only in exercise physiology but in sport sociology, psychology, philosophy, and history as well.

Although analytic thinking and rigorous data collection are becoming a reality at the top of the profession's structure, it is uncertain how much is dribbling down to the action level—i.e., the conduct of physical education. Considerable attention has recently been drawn to "bridging the gap" between the theory-research enterprise and practice. Locke has popularized the middleman concept which is intended to develop professionals whose specialty is transforming theory and research into practice [11]. Unfortunately, the middleman is not a very popular position because neither side fully appreciates his mission. Nevertheless the introduction of this concept and other similar efforts—e.g., Anne Rothstein's *Bridging the Gap* newsletter and AAHPER meetings which have focused on this task—represent a departure from earlier thought in the field and can be taken as signs of progress.

Concern for children is nothing new in the physical education literature; the education-through-the-physical advocates always reflected this concern in their arguments. However, it is encouraging to observe a number of recent articles in *JOHPER* and elsewhere written in a humanistic vein by young physical educators. Charles Schmidt's "Education for a Human Physically Interacting Society" is typical:

> Man, with sad results, has long been trying to deal both intellectually and emotionally with the problems of aggressiveness, fear, and anxiety that lead to inhumanity, hostility, and eventually war. What good we might have produced if in our activities we directed the great personal dedication so often found in our teachers to making every lesson one that teaches human respect for ourselves and others. [21]

*CHANGE IN SPORT*

Sport too has felt the pressures of change. The most widely publicized and most radical efforts to change sport and particularly intercollegiate athletics has come from Jack Scott's athletics for athletes protest which has all the distinctive signs of a social movement. Scott, operating out of the University of California at Berkeley in a loose coalition with both Harry Edwards' black athletes movement and student peace groups, started with a book published underground, *Athletics for Athletes* [22], and with a course, Intercollegiate Athletics and Education: A Social-Psychological Evaluation, taught during the 1970 winter term at Berkeley. The book has already been revised and republished by a major publishing company, this time under the title *The Athletic Revolution* [23]. Before accepting a position at Oberlin College, Scott institutionalized the movement by creating the nonprofit Institute for the Study of Sport and Society which held seminars and published a newsletter.

Scott's protest is aimed primarily at the coach-dominated athletic structure which stresses the product—i.e., winning— over the process —i.e., the experience, which is spectator- rather than participant-oriented, which serves as the training ground for "molding young boys into citizens who will be rubber stamps for the on-going social fiction," which excludes many potential participants, and, above all, which fails to fulfill the major purposes of sport: "self-expression, self-development, and enjoyment." Other topics, such as the extensive authority of the coach and current amateurism policies, also fall within Scott's purview. Herbert Kohl's foreword to Scott's first book expresses the feeling of the movement:

> It is not possible for young people to run or play games in school. No, they must be controlled, moved according to the coaches' notions of what is best for them, and they must be taught to compete, compete, compete. Winning is the substitute for experiencing joy in the movement of one's body. [22]

Intercollegiate athletics bear the brunt of Scott's attack, but his extensive criticism spills over to situations in high school and beyond. As is typical of social movement leaders, Scott bases his protest on fact but exaggerates certain situations and omits others to create a less objective but more effective picture of what he feels to be a monster that needs to be contained or slain.

The literature surrounding Scott's movement has swollen from one underground book to a number of books and articles both about the movement and about the absurdities of professional and intercollegiate athletics. One of the most popular of these has been former St. Louis Cardinal linebacker Dave Meggyesy's *Out of Their League,* a frontal attack on the inhumanity which, according to Meggyesy, runs rampant in professional football [12].

Although Scott's movement has received more attention than other hints of change in sport, alternatives to the traditional value orientations are making their appearance, albeit subtly, with increasing frequency. Super-Hippie's Peace Pentathlon [9] has already been cited as an effort by an excellent athlete to compete without "putting anyone down." Competition against others is alien to man's best interests, but competition against self is a rewarding, uplifting experience. Marathoner Kenny Moore's recent explanation of why distance runners continue to run shows the proximity of the views of many runners to the counter-culture: they disdain instrumental reasons such as medals and trophies in favor of the intrinsic feelings of the run:

> The rewards of cross-country may be unrelated to competitive success. This is not to say that one cannot derive satisfaction from winning, but if competition is the runner's only goal, he is clearly deranged. He would pursue Sophia Loren for her money, order Russian caviar for its protein content. [16]

*Sports Illustrated* is carrying increasingly more articles critical of sport's prevailing values ranging from the hair issue to this quotation from Yukio Mishima's "Testament of a Samurai":

> Even today my memory is fresh with the sorrow I felt as a boy because I thought my not having been endowed with athletic skill or strength shut me out forever from the world of sport. How fine it would be if there were even one school that did away with all varsity competition and instead so improved the status of its athletic clubs that they embraced everyone and were so run that the particular capabilities of each student were given the proper scope for development. [15]

The broadening of the scope of athletic programs is not a new source of contention in physical education, but a popular magazine's coverage of this issue is a new line of development. A dozen other recent *Sports Illustrated* articles—e.g., the "Black Athlete" series [18], the "Desperate Coach" series [27], "Is a Mustache just Peanuts?" [3]—as well as articles in other magazines such as *Look*'s "Big-Time Football Is on the Skids" [19] further illustrate the increased exposure of the public to emergent values in sport, including humanism.

James Duthie has analyzed the relationship of sport and athletics to the counter-culture [5]. In his view, athletics have developed in response to the values of the technological society with its emphasis on consumption and goal- rather than means-orientation. Sport, on the other hand, reflects the counter-culture's "spontaneous or unreflective behaviour." In athletics, pleasure derives from achieving a specific goal such as winning or properly executing a particular maneuver. The coach operates as the society's functionary to convert the spontaneous and un-reflected behavior of a young man into "responses that are deliberate, rational, and end-motivated above all," thereby "achieving society's aspirations for the athlete." To guarantee that this process operates effectively, the coach must ensure that happiness for the athlete is synonymous with "meeting achievement criteria, his production schedule." Duthie refers to Alan Sillitoe's *The Loneliness of the Long Distance Runner* as an illustration of the resolution of this conflict in favor of the counter-culture. In the story, the runner refuses to cross the finish line after arriving there ahead of the other boys; he is, in Duthie's words:

> the apotheosis of all individuals who insist on taking part in sport as a means of self-expression, who resist the shift to athletics.

Duthie's point of view further illustrates the challenge that increasingly faces traditional modes of sport in American society.

A final change in the world of sport has already been described in Chapter four—i.e., the breakdown of traditional sex roles as women begin to make their presence known in sport.

## Summary

Physical education contains many potentialities for man's social and emotional well-being. Forces in the American society have constrained these potentialities from becoming realities, but the prospects for change indicate that the gap between potentialities and realities can be narrowed.

Sociologist Wilbert Moore has persuasively argued that the rate of change is accelerating in the world and that the proportion of both planned and unplanned change is much higher now than at any other time [17]. This observation is borne out in most assessments of the emerging values in the American culture; in the increasing adoption of humanistic approaches to both academic disciplines and educational practices, despite the bleak prospects for educational change; in physical education scholarship; and in sport, where traditional values are being challenged more vigorously than ever before. Man's capacity to reflect on his culture and to change it is becoming more and more apparent. Norms and institutions today have greater flexibility and more fluctuations. Change in one part of the system affects other dimensions of the system. An increased rate of change and a shrinking world both act to encourage the adoption of elements from other cultures. The social movement is still a viable agent for change. Even revolution is part of everyday rhetoric, as Jack Scott has demonstrated in the title of his book, *The Athletic Revolution*.

Obviously, this chapter has not cited every reference which documents the proposition that physical education has become more scholarly or that traditional values in sport are under large-scale attack. The literature that has been cited simply illustrates what I feel to be a trend toward change. If the society in general and sport and physical education specifically are undergoing widespread changes and those changes are in the direction of reducing the impact of the constraining forces in the culture, then the time for the implementation of a truly humanistic physical education may be at hand.

What is needed now, at a time when change is almost commonplace and traditional values are being questioned on several fronts, is a united effort by the profession to define, adopt, and implement an approach to physical education that truly meets the needs of young and old, skilled and awkward, male and female. If the money and energy that has been spent defining a body of knowledge and publicizing the benefits of physical education (e.g., the PEPI Project) could be redirected toward this goal, then a humanistic physical education could become a reality. This kind of effort would have to lean heavily not only on the profession's commitment to mankind, but on its ability to conceptualize and to apply theory and research to the conduct of physical education.

# References

1. Bidney, David. "The Varieties of Human Freedom." In *The Concept of Freedom in Anthropology,* edited by David Bidney, pp. 11–34. The Hague: Mouton, 1963.
2. Bronowski, J. "Protest—Past and Present." *The American Scholar,* XXXVIII (Autumn 1969), 535–46.
3. Brown, Gwilym S. "Is a Mustache just Peanuts?" *Sports Illustrated,* XXXIV (June 14, 1971), 38–43.
4. Caldwell, Stratton F. "The Human Potential Movement: Origin, Emergence and Relationship of Physical Education." Paper presented at CAHPER Conference, Oakland, California, April 1–6, 1971. Dittoed.
5. Duthie, James H. "Sport: A Component of the Counter-Culture." Paper presented at the American Sociological Association Annual Meeting, Denver, Colorado, August 30, 1971. Mimeographed.
6. Fantini, Mario, and Weinstein, Gerald, eds. *Toward Humanistic Education: A Curriculum of Affect.* New York: Praeger Publishers, Inc., 1970.
7. Glass, John F. "The Humanistic Challenge to Sociology." *Journal of Humanistic Psychology,* XI (Fall 1971), 170–83.
8. "Jeremiah of Jock Liberation." *Time* (May 24, 1971), pp. 88–89.

9.  Jones, R. F. "The World's First Peace Pentathlon." *Sports Illustrated*, XXXII (May 11, 1970), 50–58.

10. Kimball, William L. "Mental Health and Selective Detachment from Culture." University of California at Los Angeles. n. d. Mimeographed.

11. Locke, Lawrence F. *Research in Physical Education.* New York: Teachers College Press, 1969.

12. Meggyesy, Dave. *Out of Their League.* Berkeley: Ramparts, 1970.

13. Miles, Matthew B. "Innovation in Education: Some Generalizations." In *Innovation in Education,* edited by Mathew B. Miles, pp. 631–62. New York: Bureau of Publications, Teachers College, 1964.

14. Miller, Richard I. "An Overview of Educational Change." In *Perspectives on Educational Change,* edited by Richard I. Miller, pp. 1–20. New York: Appleton-Century-Crofts, 1967.

15. Mishima, Yukio. "Testament of a Samurai." *Sports Illustrated,* XXXIV (January 11, 1971), 24–27.

16. Moore, Kenny. "One of the Pleasures of My Life." *Sports Illustrated,* XXXV (November 1, 1971), 53.

17. Moore, Wilbert E. *Social Change.* Englewood Cliffs, N.J.: Prentice-Hall, Inc., 1963.

18. Olsen, Jack. *The Black Athlete: A Shameful Story.* New York: Time-Life Books, 1968.

19. Padwe, Sandy. "Big-Time Football Is on the Skids." *Look* (September 22, 1970), pp. 66–69.

20. Reich, Charles A. *The Greening of America.* New York: Random House, Inc., 1970.

21. Schmidt, Charles. "Education for a Humane Physically Interacting Society." *JOHPER,* XLIII (January 1972), 33 ff.

22. Scott, Jack. *Athletics for Athletes.* Oakland: Other Ways, 1969.

23. Scott, Jack. *The Athletic Revolution.* New York: The Free Press, 1971.

24. Shecter, Leonard. "The Coming Revolt of the Athletes." *Look* (July 28, 1970), pp. 43–47.

25. Siedentop, Daryl. *Physical Education: Introductory Analysis.* Dubuque: William C. Brown Company, Publishers, 1972.

26. Staude, John Raphael. "Theoretical Foundations for a Humanistic Sociology." Paper presented at the American Sociological Association Annual Meeting, Denver, Colorado, September, 1971. Dittoed.

27. Underwood, John. "The Desperate Coach." *Sports Illustrated,* XXXI (August 25–September 8, 1969).

28. Van Dalen, D. B. "The Anatomy of Change." *Physical Educator,* XXIV (March 1967), 3–6.

29. Weinberg, Carl, ed. *Humanistic Foundations of Education.* Englewood Cliffs, N.J.: Prentice-Hall, Inc., 1972.

# 6

# Methodology
# for Implementing
# a Humanistic
# Physical Education
# Program

## Introduction

This chapter represents a significant departure from the text which has preceded it. The first five chapters attempted to develop a humanistic perspective for physical education; this chapter is concerned with methodological suggestions for implementing this point of view. The difficulty of this task is compounded by our initial umbrella-like definition of a physical education program as "any organized effort to structure learning or development over a specified period of time which focuses on large muscle physical performance." Even if we exclude patterns of physical activity in this chapter, it is apparent that most methodological considerations will be stretched to the breaking point if they are forced to fit all physical education programs. Therefore, some of the suggestions will apply only to school programs while others will be more broadly relevant. Although physical activity patterns will not be discussed, humanistic patterns will be an outgrowth of humanistic programs.

A physical educator's output—e.g., his goals and teaching methods —is dependent upon, but not necessarily predictable from, the input he receives—e.g., experiences, reading, conversations, observations. The way in which he integrates the input into his behavior is unique, but his output is affected in some way by input. Further, humanistic professional behavior is presumably based at least fifty percent on perspective. If a physical educator adopts a particular perspective, he is at least half way toward changing his professional behavior. The other half is methodology input—exposure to a variety of means to accomplish self-esteem enhancement, self-actualization, and other humanistic goals in a physical education program. Adopting a particular perspective without knowing the necessary methods to implement the goals of the new point of view can be frustrating. However, in many cases, full understanding of a new perspective opens methodological doors without the formal exposure to humanistic methods. This chapter is an effort to provide some exposure to humanistic methodology.

## School Programs

Introducing a humanistic physical education program in the schools is not easy. With the exception of varsity and extramural programs, physical education in many schools has earned a reputation as little more than regimented recess or recreation, and a physical educator who wishes to dispel this notion takes on a formidable task. A simple announcement that things are going to be different may raise a few eyebrows but isn't likely to shift students smoothly into unfamiliar behavior patterns. Repetitive announcements and discussions about the goals of the program have an aggregate effect: after about two weeks someone finally says "It looks like this might be a little different!" After a month or more the message finally takes effect. It is crucial at this stage that the teacher have a reservoir of patience in order to see the changes through.

Other factors hamper the implementation of a truly instructional program. Primary among these is the threat of grades. As long as students feel threatened, they will not learn or grow much. Teachers may be able to coerce students into moving toward goals they have set for the students, but fear leaves a scar, especially for those students who never convinced themselves that they fully accomplished the goals or who failed to achieve the goals in the eyes of the teacher. Moreover, some students who feel threatened simply refuse to play the game and become a "no suit" bystander. Since the abolishment of grades as a way of life is not practical for most schools at this time, an alternative to evaluating according to achievement or improvement is presented here.

A grade based entirely on student involvement, often referred to as effort or "attitude," would award an "A" (or whatever the highest grade happens to be) for attending and putting forth a good effort regularly. This, in combination with sound instruction and individualized goals, would both reduce the threat of grades since everyone would possess the capability for meeting the highest standard and, importantly, encourage a high rate of self-development. Assuming that the student attended and produced a good effort regularly, improvement in accordance with his abilities would be guaranteed if sound instruction were provided. Attendance is easily measured, and effort is continually monitored subjectively by the teacher even if records are not kept. Of course, some artificiality is introduced into the system if the student must demonstrate good effort toward a goal in which he has no interest. This problem will be considered later in the chapter. Another alternative to grading involves gradually turning the responsibility for evaluation over to the students. This approach is described later in the chapter along with other individualizing procedures.

For different reasons, some of which are linked to grading, many students view school as a place they would rather not be if they had their choice. Parents are often blamed for current discipline problems, and perhaps they can be blamed for failing to encourage a positive attitude toward school. The fact remains that school is too often a place where children either fail or have experiences which are not meaningful to them. In either case, their frustration with the system leads to disruptive behavior. For many, even the threat of grades carries no weight; grades only act as rewards for those who still desire to operate within the school system. Although there are still other students who desire to succeed in school but who have failed in physical education, the key issue in this discussion is whether physical education can divorce itself from those characteristics of school which created these frustrations in the first place.

Although the subject matter of physical education differs from other school subjects many of the trappings are the same. Achievement, rather than student involvement, is often used as the major criterion for evaluation. Written tests remind students of other classes. Rules abound: don't chew gum, wear regulation gym clothing and shoes, don't talk here or there, take showers—all of which are strongly reminiscent of a middle-class parent-child orientation which many students associate with school but which, because of their family and neighborhood experiences, they have never understood. The command style of teaching is also a favorite with physical educators; several physical education majors who recently observed over ten physical education teachers in two different school districts came to me to ask where they could go to observe something other than the command method. The popularity of this teaching style is important to note because complete authority and responsibility are vested in the teacher in the command approach; student opinions are not considered.

There is much that gets in the way of learning and, significantly, of the joy of physical activity in many schools. The head of a high school physical education department recently said: "By high schoool I think we manage to kill the interest in activity for about ninety percent of the students." If we are really interested in igniting the interest of those who have been disenchanted with school, we must reduce competitive achievement as the only standard of excellence, rules oriented toward middle-class uniformity, and classroom tactics and authoritarian teaching techniques, none of which are necessarily central to the subject matter of physical education.

Two concepts receiving considerable attention in educational circles are accountability and behavioral objectives. Both are more concerned with educational goals than the methods by which the goals are reached, but both have rather clear implications for methodology. Accountability means that the teacher is accountable for student learning. In a sense, this is nothing new; the literature is filled with efforts to define effective teaching by identifying criteria that can be applied to all teachers. What is new is the shift from teacher behavior to student behavior: if the student does not learn, the teacher, no matter how impressive his manner and methods, will be judged ineffectual. Closely linked to accountability is the concept of behavioral or, more accurately, performance objectives in which measurable learning outcomes are specifically spelled out. The implication that only those goals which are amenable to measurement will qualify as performance objectives has caused considerable criticism of this concept, because many objectives, particularly humanistic ones, do not lend themselves to accurate measurement. In turn, proponents of performance objectives have allowed crude indices of achievement to substitute for accurate measurement for those objectives which cannot be accurately measured. For example, if participation during adult leisure time were an objective of a tennis program for adolescents, perhaps simply asking the students whether they think they will play tennis later in life could be used to gain some idea of whether the objective is being met.

The effect of both accountability and performance objectives on teaching methodology is to shift attention to the learner and his needs in relation to a specific objective for which the teacher is held accountable. This change in emphasis from teacher to learner, while frustrating for the teacher who feels that his methodology is sound but that some students just don't want to learn, tends to loosen teaching methodology to the extent that the teacher recognizes that each learner may achieve the same objective in a slightly different way and in a different length of time. Although individualized instruction is not an automatic outcome of the adoption of accountability and performance objectives, these concepts tend to widen the process of learning while focusing on a specific measurable objective.

There is no question that the application of these concepts could easily become abusive. For one thing, teachers do not all aim for the same objectives; they are guided by their academic backgrounds and personal strengths and weaknesses. For another, teachers cannot be held uniformly accountable unless the groups of students are comparable. Therefore, some educators have advocated involving the individual teacher in the process of deciding what objectives are feasible for his programs and his students that particular year and how they are to be measured. This approach individualizes the whole procedure, not just the methodology. However, this approach still limits student-initiated objectives. If an eventual goal is to turn over to the student complete responsibility for his own learning, then at some time he will begin to determine his own objectives. It may be that accountability can be shifted to the learner so that he is held accountable for the performance objectives that he has constructed.

# Teaching Styles

Muska Mosston's provocative book *Teaching Physical Education: From Command to Discovery* [24] describes a spectrum of teaching styles which are characterized by the extent of control retained by the teacher in three stages of the teaching process: preclass decisions, the execution stage, and evaluation of the learners' performance. Each teaching style is further evaluated by the extent of its contribution to four developmental channels: biological, psychological, social, and cognitive. In general, Mosston's thesis is that the command style in which the teacher retains complete control of all preclass decisions (the plan for the day), the execution of the lesson (lecture, demonstration, and who is to move where, when, and for how long), and the evaluation of everyone's performance that day is not only the typical pattern for teaching physical education but it also contributes least to each of the four developmental channels. He therefore proceeds to describe teaching styles which progressively turn control over to the students, particularly in the execution and evaluation stages, and which, by his assessment, increasingly contribute to the four developmental channels.

Mosston's work represents a significant departure from most teaching methods literature in physical education not only because he has criticized a style of teaching upon which most physical educators have relied but also because he has offered real alternatives supported by extensive examples. However, Mosston leans heavily on the cognitive developmental channel and fails to loosen his hold on preclass decisions, even in his problem-solving teaching style which, other than a brief reference to creativity as another style, is the most progressive teaching style in his spectrum. Mosston's bias toward cognitive development is countered in this text by a bias toward social and emotional growth. However, since such growth is at least partly dependent upon the actualization of physical potentialities, it is necessary to investigate the effectiveness of the command teaching style in comparison to more individualized approaches before describing individualized instruction as a teaching style.

Bloom's taxonomy of educational objectives [3] categorizes the kinds of learning that can occur in physical education programs: the psychomotor domain (referred to in this text as physical ability) includes both motor skill development and physical fitness development, the cognitive domain encompasses at least rules and strategies, and the affective domain covers the behavioral or social-emotional objectives. Much of this text has focused on the effect of psychomotor development on affective development; any discussion of the effectiveness of a particular teaching method must, following this line of thought, pay attention to the psychomotor domain. Some physical educators who advocate individualized instruction and denigrate the command style point out that while their approach may not teach motor skills as well, their concern is less with motor skill development than with developing individual initiative, responsibility, and the ability to make decisions relevant to the self. Implementing humanistic goals as described in this book requires methods which ensure both kinds of development.

Physical fitness development (as one aspect of the psychomotor domain) would probably not be handicapped by more individualized teaching methods, because the kinds of learning that are involved are primarily cognitive (such as using pulse rate and time to control the intensity of aerobic work) in combination with the development of a training program. Both the cognitive and skill components (such as foot and arm mechanics in jogging or body position in weight training) can be taught in a group in short sessions. The major thrust of such a program, however, could easily consist of an individualized training pattern suited to the student's needs, abilities, and interests. We will return to this point later; it is sufficient here to note that the case for the command approach would be precarious if it were promoted as a superior method for developing physical fitness.

Since the affective domain is treated at some length later in this chapter, it only remains to investigate the other aspect of the psychomotor domain, motor skill development, in relation to the command style of teaching. The question, then, is: Does the command approach, in comparison to more individualized teaching methods, more effectively facilitate the learning of a motor skill? Humanists such as Earle Kelley have argued that if teachers can provide a nonthreatening environment which acts to "open selves" and then have something around for students to learn, they will learn [16]. John Holt, in *How Children Learn,* has even proposed that children learn sports more effectively by themselves without any professional instruction [13]. An alternative hypothesis, derived from my observation of, and experimentation with, a variety of teaching methods, is that the teacher who has his students working on different motor skills at different levels has difficulty assisting the progress of each student. While he works with one student or a small group of students, others may be learning on their own, but still others are incorporating errors into their performance. For example, two students who are working on the tennis backhand may not be meeting the ball far enough in front of the body. If they do not perceive this error on their own, they will continue to make contact with the ball incorrectly until it becomes part of an established motor pattern. In the command style of teaching, even with a heterogeneous group which contains several levels of ability, everyone works on the tennis backhand at the same time, enabling the instructor to discuss common problems with the entire group as well as to supervise one specific motor skill for errors and adjustments. The extent of difficulty of individual instruction hinges at least partly on the extent of individualization. If everyone is working on tennis skills of some kind at one level or another, the difficulty of providing feedback for each student is reduced; if three of four activities are going at once, each with a variety of skills and ability levels, attention to correct motor patterns is more difficult.

Perhaps programed instruction is a solution to this dilemma, as Lawrence Locke and Mary Jensen have pointed out, but programed instruction in physical education is in its infancy and many of the problems have yet to be solved. [19]. Then, too, programed instruction usually assumes a minimum capability to read and to transfer movements on a written page or on film to one's own movements. Mosston and others have advocated task cards which list specific movements of increasing difficulty, but again the learner must be able to perceive his own movements in relation to the written word. Even a task such as climbing a rope, which has several possible solutions, will necessitate personal instruction and assistance for some students. In an effort to remedy this difficulty, the Omaha public schools have adopted a physical education program which combines the use of task cards, reference books, loop films, and videotape with self, peer, and teacher prescription, evaluation, and diagnosis [33].

The hypothesis that motor skills are more readily learned through individualized instruction than by the command method has been tested a few times in the literature—e.g., the tennis skills studies by Joan Farrell [7], Tom Mariani [23], and Donna Rae Marburger [22]; a volleyball skills study by Robert Allen [2]; and motor skills studies by Roy Keller [15], Neil Dougherty [5], and Thomas Vodola [34]—without clearly demonstrating the effectiveness of either the command approach or more individualized styles of teaching. However, most of these studies used voluntary subjects; involuntary subjects (e. g., from public schools) may respond differently. The most supportive study for the command approach was directed by Joan Manahan using seventh-grade girls in an archery unit [21]. She found that the group which received specific instructions concerning the performance of archery skills improved significantly more than the group which was allowed to explore these skills on an individual basis, receiving instructor feedback only when they requested it. Certain students in the individualized group did quite well on their own, but the average improvement of the individualized group was less and for at least one student who never seemed to perceive her problems, the improvement was negligible.

Of course all discussion about whether the command style better facilitates motor skill learning than more individualized methods makes little sense if the motor skill under consideration is not meaningful to the student. Although voluntary programs do not have this problem, schools usually require their students to take certain courses and these courses, in turn, often require students to accomplish certain tasks. The humanistic view of educational psychology, as articulated in depth by Carl Weinberg and Philip Reidford [35], holds that the student is better able to determine his own learning style as well as what is most meaningful for him to learn.

Just as students differ, so, too, do teachers. One instructor may excel at demonstrating a particular skill, another is more comfortable in a one-to-one teaching situation, a third finds his greatest moments in organizing a program, and still another may be more adept at teaching the highly skilled. For those physical educators who excel at group demonstrations, lectures, and discussions and at planning and evaluating on a group basis, the command style of teaching fits well. Unfortunately, both because the command approach has had widespread acceptance and because it offers some protection from getting close to students, it is currently being used by many physical educators who do not excel in command methodology. Still, what is most comfortable for the instructor may not meet the needs of the students—a major difficulty of the command style even for a physical educator who performs these tasks effectively. This style not only assumes that the instructor knows what is best for the students but also that preclass decisions will be applicable to the entire group. It is well suited to the essentialists in physical education—those teachers who believe that certain principles and skills should be dogmatically taught to everyone.

The extent to which the command approach can effectively meet the needs of a group depends in part on the homogeneity of the group. If the group contains both high and low skilled students, an instructor using the command style will often "shoot for the middle," thus aiming preclass decisions and lesson execution at one target. His target group will therefore be somewhat narrower than the group he is supposed to be addressing. The usual result is that the high skilled become bored while the low skilled struggle to keep up. These same students crop up as problems in applying specific evaluation criteria which, again, were developed for a narrow target group.

If it is true that the more homogeneous the group in needs, abilities, and interests, the fewer deviations there will be from the target group, then students ought to be placed into homogeneous groups whenever possible. However, two kinds of problems emerge in grouping. First, it is extremely difficult to group students according to their needs, abilities, and interests, either in the public school (even with modular scheduling) or in private programs, especially if we are really interested in identifying and taking into account student needs such as self-esteem, student interests such as the variety of meanings they attach to different activities, and the wide range of student abilities. We usually settle instead for some crude division based on ability or observable motivation.

The second problem, particularly germane to public school programs, involves the effect of grouping on the low ability group. Unfortunately, very little research has focused on physical education grouping. Janet Seaman's study, one of the few efforts to determine the effects of ability grouping on physical education students, found that physically disabled students preferred the regular class in comparison to an adapted program [30]. Two literature reviews of academic grouping cited by Thomas Vodola [34] concluded that ability grouping is not particularly advantageous. After gathering data from two schools and reviewing a number of other academic tracking studies, Schafer and his associates concluded that students in the low track get worse academically, become worse discipline problems, come from lower socio-economic backgrounds, and tend to remain in the low track, and that teachers of low track students expect less and are less inspired [29]. On the other hand, Miriam Goldberg and her associates' investigation of the influence of ability grouping on self-esteem revealed that, in general, ability grouping positively affected the self-attitudes of low ability students but had the reverse effect on high ability students [10]. This cursory review of literature serves to illustrate the problematic effects of ability grouping on students.

William Glasser, in *Schools Without Failure,* favors homogeneous grouping only when students have both academic and discipline problems and then only on a temporary basis until some progress is made [9]. Dual grouping, a similar approach which places students in a special group only part of the time may reduce some of the disadvantages of grouping, but once again the physical educator is faced with developing valid criteria for admission to the special group. Optional grouping, which gives students a choice of joining a special group such as an obesity program or which is oriented toward specific short-term interests such as strength development for beginners, is probably most in line with humanistic thought. In this method students are allowed to connect their own needs, abilities, and interests to available programs. This, of course, assumes considerable self-understanding on the part of the student, a matter addressed later in this chapter.

Although the issue of the command style's effectiveness has not been resolved, there are serious reservations to its use if humanistic goals are adopted. Even the motor skills question has not been answered in a manner which clearly supports the command approach. Therefore, we must turn to other teaching styles in order to explore their effectiveness in facilitating humanistic goals.

Mosston's extremely detailed account of the spectrum of teaching styles, emphasizing cognitive development, can be consulted [24] for a more complete description of a variety of teaching styles. Our discussion will follow the progression from the command approach to more individualized methods of teaching physical education which are designed to facilitate humanistic goals. We will illustrate each successive move away from the command approach with a specific physical ability task, i.e., the push-up.

(1) If an instructor were to teach the push-up using the command style, his preclass decisions would involve how he was going to present the push-up and how the students were to learn and develop in relation to his presentation. In the execution stage, he would show them how to do a correct push-up and then guide and supervise them as a group in doing a specified number of push-ups at his command. The evaluation would consist of determining the extent to which each student performed in accordance with his instructions. (2) Probably the first alteration of the command style in a progression toward individualization would be to allow the students to execute the specified number of push-ups at their own rate. Thus individualization would be increased by taking into consideration differences in the time it takes students to complete a task. Everything else—the preclass decisions, the presentation, the number of push-ups to be executed, the evaluation—would remain the same, but, importantly, some responsibility would be turned over to the students. (3) If further individualization were desired, the next step would be to allow the students to determine not only the rate but also the number of push-ups they need to do. This further individualizes by recognizing not only different levels of upper body muscular endurance but also different goals within the narrow framework of push-ups. Student decisions concerning their own goals could form a separate teaching style if it does not seem desirable to individualize both the level of muscular endurance and the goal of such an experience at the same time. This approach also implies a subtle change in the evaluation procedure, since it logically follows that increases in a student's number of push-ups would be based on the student's evaluation of his own progress. However, all other responsibilities would remain in the instructor's hands.

(4) To this point the shift in responsibilities can be categorized in Mosston's words, as, "quantitative differentiation" [24]. The next teaching style begins to encompass "qualitative differentiation"—that

is, the student is allowed to choose the kind of push-up that best suits his needs and abilities as well as the rate and number. To accomplish this requires a slight change in another part of the execution stage: the instructor must present a number of alternative forms of push-ups such as knee push-ups, wall push-ups, and let-downs for weaker students; feet-elevated push-ups and extension presses for stronger students; and push-ups with hands at various widths for different kinds of development. He still controls preclass decisions in this teaching style, at least to the extent that all students are required to do some form of push-up, but once again students are responsible for setting goals and for evaluating their own progress. (5) In the next approach, students become responsible for another qualitative decision: a choice of upper body muscular endurance exercises. In this approach, the instructor's preclass decision is loosened so that only the general goal of upper body muscular endurance remains. To meet this goal, a variety of exercises such as push-ups, pull-ups, dips, weight training, and isometrics are presented as options for the student to consider in planning and evaluating his own upper body muscular endurance program.

(6) To further individualize, the instructor's preclass decisions can be reduced to the general goal of physical fitness. Students would decide whether and to what extent upper body muscular endurance is relevant to their fitness needs, and how they should accomplish this goal if they decide to include it. The execution stage would widen the options once more, this time by including a presentation of other fitness possibilities such as aerobic capacity, muscular strength, and flexibility, each accompanied by means to achieve that goal—for example, jogging and interval training to improve aerobic capacity. Students would be placed in charge of developing their own fitness programs and evaluating their own progress. (7) Finally, the preclass decisions would be entirely shifted to the students so that they could plan, execute, and evaluate their own physical education program according to their own needs, abilities, and interests with the instructor providing guidance and suggestions at all three stages—preclass decisions, execution, and evaluation—without preempting the student's decisions and actions.

These seven teaching styles represent a progression which not only increasingly becomes individualized but which can be viewed as a step-by-step loosening of the sort of superstructure that most students have experienced for years. The instructor does not adopt one of the seven teaching styles but instead starts with the command approach and progressively shifts responsibility to the students as they grow in their awareness of physical education and its relation to their lives—i.e., self-understanding—as well as in self-esteem and self-actualization as physical education students.

Other examples could be substituted for the push-up which, admittedly, represents physical fitness development rather than motor skill development. Using soccer rather than the push-up to illustrate the spectrum of teaching styles, the instep kick could be taught with one or two specific drills controlled and evaluated by the teacher, followed by students drilling without strict supervision, students constructing their own drills, students starting with heading or trapping or even strategy as they see fit, students selecting from among several team sports or from several "imported" sports, and, finally, students developing, executing, and evaluating their own physical education programs.

This sequence of teaching styles assumes that all students will progress at the same rate in accepting responsibility for their own actions and in developing a sufficient knowledge base with which to make decisions. In reality, students progress at different rates; therefore, more than one teaching style may be necessary at one time. It has been my experience that most students can function comfortably and effectively in relation to their own needs and abilities within one progressively individualized teaching style. However, a few students need more guidance, and a few can be released more quickly. These cases can be treated individually by finding the appropriate teaching style for these students.

Another possibility, described by Mosston and others, is to devise a variety of task cards which list specific tasks in sequence. This plan organizes the options for students so that they can choose a particular task and a particular level within that task. It is based on A.M. Gentile's model for skill acquisition which sets goals but allows students to formulate their own motor plan to achieve the goal (task) [8]. Task cards assume that students can evaluate and correct their motor plan in order to accomplish the task. The range of tasks available to students would depend on the teaching style adopted by the instructor.

A frequent criticism of individualized instruction in physical education is that students select what they already do quite well, and therefore physical education becomes a recess period. This kind of freedom to select rests upon several assumptions: a nonthreatening environment which encourages students to experiment with the unknown, a step-by-step education in the process of decision-making in physical education, a professional physical educator to make the options clear and to provide the appropriate guidance, and, most importantly, self-esteem and self-understanding as a physical education student as well as the beginning of self-actualization. Some physical educators, in an effort to counteract a student's earlier negative experiences with a particular activity, say "Try it our way before you make a final decision." This approach encourages some exposure to all activities before developing a personalized program.

I have had the opportunity to implement the progressively individualized style of teaching with 29 high school freshman boys, about a third of whom could be considered disadvantaged. I had an advantage —I was assigned an assistant, a senior in high school; but my program had to fit a rather traditional three-week unit schedule. Since physical fitness is easier to individualize, fitness was scheduled twice a week. By the tenth week, the students were writing their own programs and carrying out these programs on their own. A few students did not develop a sufficient knowledge base according to their answers in our weekly discussions, but they were given guidance in these matters. Since motor skills were taught in three-day per week, three-week units, it was difficult to improve skills. However, task cards were used as well as voluntary grouping ("who would like to learn how to pass a football correctly?") which appeared to meet the needs of more students. Student attitudes were quite positive, to the point that other teachers began to get inquiries from their students about our program. The program is still in progress, but by the last month of the school year I am certain that at least three-quarters of the students will be entirely on their own, selecting their own goals (fitness, motor skills, or some combination) as well as methods to reach these goals.

We have yet to treat self-esteem, self-actualization, self-understanding, and interpersonal relations methodologically, but before we do, we need to summarize the humanistic benefits of individualized instruction beyond any effects this method of teaching has on these four concepts. Individualized instruction is based on the proposition that each student is a unique individual with unique needs, abilities, interests, and feelings, who knows better than anyone else what makes sense to him and what is most meaningful in his life. If his feelings are uniquely his and if his potentialities are unique to him, only an individual program with himself as the chief consultant can fully meet his needs and actualize his potentialities.

## Self-Esteem

In order to enhance self-esteem in a physical education setting, at least three conditions are necessary: a nonthreatening environment, treatment of each student as a unique and special individual, and opportunities for success. Individualized instruction contributes to each of these conditions, but there are other factors including the competencies of the teacher, the content of the curriculum, the facility itself, and special projects initiated for this purpose.

It should be obvious that the instructor is central to everything else that goes on. An excellent curriculum with a mediocre staff quickly becomes a mediocre program. In many instances, the instructor determines curriculum, modifies facilities, and initiates special projects. Further, because of the strong connection between perceived physical ability development and self-perceptions, the instructor must be competent to teach the subject matter within physical education for which he is responsible. When we speak of physical ability development, nothing can substitute for sound instruction.

Beyond this kind of competency as a physical educator, there are at least three crucial characteristics which will aid in the students' development of positive self-esteem. The first characteristic is sensitivity to student needs, abilities, interests, and feelings along with the understanding that these are unique to each individual. Some instructors pay more attention to how students feel about what is going on than others and are careful about placing a student in a situation which may be embarrassing to him because of an ability or interest gap; others assume that all of their students need a large dose of whatever they happen to be dispensing at that time without regard to individual needs. Second, the instructor must be able to demonstrate a genuine warmth and concern for students and their development. Those students who do not perceive themselves as recipients of this warmth and concern will not feel special or successful and may feel threatened. Underlying these first two characteristics is the instructor's own self-esteem. To be concerned and sensitive, the teacher must feel comfortable with himself so that he can turn his attention to others rather than focusing on what students are doing for or to him. Third, the instructor must be someone students can respect. This condition, perhaps the most difficult one to develop in a teacher, is really the basis for the others, because all the sensitivity and concern that an instructor can muster will be wasted if students do not desire to be on the receiving end of his efforts. This ability to build rapport and mutual respect with students can be characterized as a kind of charisma. It may become less important as students begin to value individuals for their uniqueness and for their feelings, but the discussion of the American culture clearly indicates the cultural limitations of this kind of development in beginning students.

In addition to characteristics of the instructor, the subject matter itself can influence self-esteem, particularly with regard to opportunities for success and the extent of threat posed by the environment. The subject matter of physical education takes many forms—e.g., team sports, physical fitness activities, aquatics, dance, ball skills, combatives, closed skills—and efforts to classify this subject matter into a few descriptive categories are numerous. If the enhancement of self-feelings is the goal, it makes sense to categorize activities according to different kinds of competition. Some activities—such as jogging, dance, movement exploration, weight training, perceptual-motor activities, and gymnastics—can be viewed primarily as competition with self; therefore the emphasis is on self-improvement—e.g., "Can I execute a forward roll?" or "Can I run farther today than I did last week?" or "Has my strength improved?" In reality, any physical activity can take this form as long as the emphasis is placed on individual improvement of a particular motor skill or physical fitness component. Only when someone tries to defeat another (e.g., sport or elimination games) or one group tries to defeat another group in a structured contest using these physical abilities does a different kind of competition emerge. However, given the current cultural values, even an activity that is structured toward self-competition may include competition with others on an informal basis—e.g., "I can run faster than you can" or "I can do more stunts than you can." It is the responsibility of the teacher to reduce this kind of competition by discussion, feedback, and positive role model behavior.

Besides competition with self, two other categories are competition with others and team competition. Although individual competition with another isolates the individual's performance, team sports not only require sufficient proficiency to play well but also the necessity of cooperating and gaining group approval. Someone whose skills are not up to the level of his teammates may find himself shunted to an out-of-the-way position, and may also be derided verbally for his failure to contribute to the team's success. Our concern here is with the development of positive physical ability self-perceptions which, for some students, must be based at least initially on self-improvement. To conclude that all competition with others is bad is to misread the intention of this methodology.

The usual concern with facilities is sufficient space and equipment. However, Muska Mosston and Rudy Mueller have pointed out a different consideration: the number of private places that are available to try out physical tasks without being scrutinized by either peers or instructors [25]. A library usually has such private places, but a gym does not. Where can a student go to try a handstand, to shoot a basket, to go through the mechanics of a throw that is not in plain view of everyone?

Could such places be constructed using drapery of some kind or collaps-ible (and expensive) handball court walls?

Another point made by Mosston and Mueller which is only tangen-tially related to the facilities issue is the matter of required clothing. The requirements of uniforms assume that each student feels comfortable in the same outfit. While certain uniforms may facilitate movement, they ignore other considerations. For example, some overweight and under-weight students may prefer to cover their entire bodies with loose-fitting clothing, and some students may prefer warmer or cooler attire. Attention to these needs will help to ensure a nonthreatening environ-ment wherein each student is treated as an individual.

Finally, a wide range of special projects can enhance self-esteem in a physical education program. Representative examples will be included here, but such projects are limited only by the imagination of the in-structor. Fantini and Weinstein have suggested a number of projects designed to buttress the feeling that "I am special" [6]. One example adapted from their work is to take a picture of each student posing in his favorite activity or in the motor skill of his choice within a particular activity and then post these pictures on a "Hall of Fame" bulletin board. The idea is nothing new; varsity sports have used this technique for years, particularly with star athletes. The difference in this project is that all students participate in an individualized experience which can then be shared by others.

A second project is one which was devised for a weeklong program involving students of both sexes aged nine to fourteen: a seven event "Olympics" with a few major alterations. To become a winner in any event it was only necessary for the student to improve his score between Monday's pretest and Friday's posttest. To prevent students from "hus-tling" the system and thereby destroying its meaning for others, the pretest was administered prior to full explanation of the rules. The events were selected according to two criteria: they had to be represen-tative of a wide range of abilities, and they had to be amenable to change in a week's time. Several of the events, such as the agility run and the stork stand on a rock (a balance test), could be improved simply by practicing on each of the three days between the pretest and posttest, because learning was a factor in performing these tasks. Other events such as the softball throw could be improved by simple drills and analyses designed to improve the mechanics of performance. Students were free to enter any or all of the events as they saw fit. Although several administrative problems arose during the week, there was over eighty percent improvement across all events. The students' verbal re-sponses to the program were even more gratifying; rather than announcing who they had beaten in a particular event, many verbalized their pride in their improvement during the week. Obviously, this project was designed to focus the participant's attention on his own development and then to provide some insurance that improvement would occur.

So much for directly influencing self-esteem development. Indirectly, however, self-esteem may be enhanced by social approval, improved social relations, and perhaps even social mobility which sometimes result from identification with and participation in certain physical education programs. Jersild has argued that such programs, particularly interscholastic athletics, should therefore be widened in order to offer these benefits to more students [14]. Methodologically this would mean providing a number of varsity athletic teams beyond the usual "feeder system" prevalent in many schools. This argument is elaborated upon as part of the self-actualization discussion.

## Self-Actualization

This book has divided physical self-actualization into three dimensions: physical ability development, self-expression, and total involvement. Physical ability development has already been recognized for its contribution to self-esteem by emphasizing the instructional competency of the teacher, but if we are really interested in identifying and developing the student's unique physical potentialities, a number of additional methodological suggestions need to be implemented.

The first of these involves young children. Although there is considerable disagreement concerning the role of perceptual-motor activities in physical education, those children who have perceptual difficulties such as body image, laterality, and directionality should be identified at an early age, and only those students who are so identified should be taught basic perceptual-motor skills, thereby providing a basis for later development. Children who have trouble with basic cultural activity skills such as throwing, running, and climbing should also be identified and helped in order to build a foundation for later development.

In addition to attention to those who have not developed basic abilities on their own, observation and testing can be used to determine unique, hidden physical potentialities of people of all ages. For example, a running start in a dash will isolate speed from acceleration, starting skills, and reaction time; by using this technique we may find a student who has good speed but who has problems with other factors associated with sprinting and therefore does not score well in a traditional dash. At least two paths are open in such a case. One is to develop those abilities which are lacking so that the student can participate and grow in one of the traditional activities. The other is to widen the boundaries of the physical education program so that unique activities are available for unique skills. If a student is found to have unusual static balance, perhaps an activity can be created to utilize and enhance this physical ability. One elementary physical education teacher recently related that each year he seems to add new events to his annual field day, because he is always finding some student who does one thing quite well, such as jumping rope, but scores poorly on all the field day events. This, of course, returns us to the self-esteem issue, since the field day plays a recognition rather than a developmental role, although it also serves to encourage further development.

Testing and observation place the burden for identifying student potentials on the teacher. Students many times can identify their own strengths and weaknesses if they are enthusiastically exposed to a wide variety of activities. A student who has been introduced by an effective teacher to gymnastics, swimming, volleyball, jogging, and modern dance has more of an opportunity to identify his potentialities than that student who has only experienced football, basketball, and baseball, or field hockey, volleyball, and softball. As individuals begin to identify those activities which are most closely associated with their own physical potentialities, more opportunities to specialize—to learn and develop and practice—are required. Nonschool programs in dance, gymnastics, aquatics, physical fitness, and a host of other activities, as well as school sport club programs help to meet this need. Unfortunately, too many required school programs are based on repeated introductory three-week units with no outlets for further development other than the traditional male varsity athletic program. How much learning really goes on in a three-week unit is one issue; another is where students whose interest is ignited can go to learn more. Offering on an elective basis advanced activities which are real advanced learning experiences rather than play and tournament time may provide an answer. Another answer, infinitely less popular, is to increase the number of extracurricular activity programs by going to a three-day–two-day coaching pattern wherein, for example, in the fall football would practice and play games on Monday, Wednesday, and Friday, while soccer, with the same coach, practiced and played on Tuesday and Thursday. This way the number of advanced activities could be doubled without adding staff. Another option is to recognize the recreational rather than learning character of intramural sports and to institute several levels of teams for each varsity sport, each with a coach and other teams to play at their level. "JV" teams and 150-pound football are examples of this approach, but the usual pattern is to group players by year in school rather than ability level, so that a senior who is not talented enough to be selected for the varsity but who has a desire to develop his athletic abilities cannot belong to the "JV."

Although this book has stressed psychosocial growth almost to the exclusion of other considerations, it is necessary at this point to describe the relationship of cognitive elements to physical ability development. In addition to perceptual-motor corrective work, measurement, exposure to a wide range of activities, and specialization, the individual should develop a sound knowledge base which will help him to actualize his potentialities. He may have identified body building as one of his potentialities, but he must possess sufficient knowledge of methods to achieve muscle definition in order to realize his potentiality. She may have the capacity for advanced floor exercise, but she must learn how to analyze her own movements in relation to a model (unless, of course, a command style teacher is always present). Physical education contains an abundance of subject matter ranging from skills and strategies to fitness concepts. Full physical ability actualization depends on a sound knowledge base in the area of specialization.

Implementation of the creative self-expression dimension of physical self-actualization involves the inclusion of self-expressive experiences in physical education programs. Typically, movement exploration and modern dance fulfill this objective, requiring sport-oriented physical educators to relinquish their tight hold on curricular offerings and to widen their view of what is masculine. Sport may also contain some potential for creative self-expression which has not been tapped due to efforts to structure all facets of sport, including the kinds of acceptable motor patterns involved in a particular task. For example, a boys' pick-up basketball game will consist of jump shots and screens either taught directly or copied from role models; there is little individual exploration of the variety of skills and strategies potentially available to them. Yet without such exploration we would not have the Fosbury Flop or Willie Mays' basket catch.

Some teachers have given their students a ball of some kind and, using Mosston's guided discovery or problem-solving method [24], have allowed them to invent their own game. In fact, Mosston's most progressive teaching style, problem-solving, contains considerable capacity for creative self-expression. In this teaching style, a specific problem is designed by the instructor and described to the students. Students then try to solve the problem by trial-and-error, either individually or in groups. The teacher may guide them in this process (guided discovery) or accept any solution that achieves the objective. A touch football unit in which rules—including the number of players—are changed on a weekly basis to force adaptation to change, problem-solving, and, hopefully, some creativity, illustrates another possibility.

To encourage total involvement in physical activity, including all of the personal feelings and meanings attached to such involvement, requires both a nonthreatening environment and an individualized program capable of offering a wide range of activities varying both in type and intensity. Only with the proper environment can all students feel free to get involved totally. Without a variety of activities the kinds of personal feelings and meanings, not to mention involvement itself, would be restricted. For example, each student may attach a different meaning to the same activity, suggesting a number of groups if interest is high, while students in activities as different as dance and baseball may experience similar feelings and meanings. One very simple method is to ask students to group themselves into more competitive and less competitive groups.

A concrete example of the incorporation of this dimension of self-actualization into a teaching methodology for instruction in a specific sport was my experimental approach to a ten-week elective handball course for college men. For the first two weeks of class it was announced that grades were to be based entirely on involvement, which essentially meant "showing up and trying." Also in that first two weeks it was announced that students could select one of three "tracks": one track was to be a highly coached, intensive learning experience including written evaluations by the instructor and a refereed tournament; a second track consisted of some group or command instruction, a few drills, and a tournament; and a third track was recreational in nature, with only minimal group instruction and no tournament. These tracks, it was announced, had nothing to do with ability level, only with interest (i.e., feelings, meanings). The announcements were repetitive because past experience suggested that students do not readily believe or participate in new ways of doing things. Only five of 24 students chose the high intensity track at first, and each had or perceived himself to have some ability. Slowly others joined, including some of the low ability students, until eleven in all were members of track one. Only one student elected the third track, and he had considerable potential as a handball player. The anonymous course evaluations at the end of the program attested to its popularity with the students, especially for tracks one and three. In fact, the lone track three student was ecstatic. There were, however, some grumbles in track two from a few students who desired more attention from the instructor (they probably chose the wrong track for them).

Methodologically, the three-track system was not difficult to implement. All students received a few minutes of instruction at the beginning of class, followed by a division into designated courts. One of the six courts was designated as a nontournament court at all times, and two courts plus one doubles squash court were designated as track one drill stations, where the instructor spent most of his time. Two separate tournaments were eventually organized; track one had the instructor as a referee on one court while the track two tournament was refereed by the players.

## *Self-Understanding*

Since self-understanding involves introspection by each student into the relationship between his needs, abilities, and interests in physical education and his life, the methodology to achieve this goal must necessarily be individualized. Therefore, many of the suggestions already made in this chapter—such as individualized teaching styles, sensitivity of the instructor, and a variety of available specialties—can supplement this process. However, at least three rather distinct aspects of self-understanding methodology should be helpful in implementing this humanistic goal: group guidance lectures and discussions, individual guidance sessions, and special projects.

Group guidance lectures and discussions simply introduce students to an awareness of some of the more common student needs, abilities, and interests in physical education and some of the more common relationships both among these variables and between them and the student's life. These group sessions can be an important part of the individualizing process; as students are given more responsibility for their own program, they should be made increasingly aware of the possible connections between the options open to them and their feelings and behavior.

I had a recent opportunity to engage in a discussion with freshman boys in physical education at a large urban high school. The session was videotaped to allow an opportunity to review what had and had not happened. The subject of the discussion was the relationship between nine recently administered physical ability tests and the factors affecting their individual decisions concerning improvement in these nine abilities. Factors such as self- and body-esteem were discussed as well as a variety of possible connections between these abilities and their present and future lives. One characteristic of the meeting was clear: it was a difficult subject for students who were used to the command approach. As a result, the discussion became a lecture except for those parts dealing with methods of improving the various test results. However, as part of this plan, a few minutes at the end of the class periods following this discussion were allotted for individualized work and help, and several students did consult me concerning needs such as losing weight and improving the mechanics of running in order to "make the track team." Although by no means a complete success, this experiment pointed out the potentialities of group guidance sessions.

Individual guidance sessions can be derivatives of group discussions as shown in the preceding example. As the program is increasingly individualized, the instructor has more time to consult individually with students. This is not an effort to create budding psychologists or psychiatrists out of physical educators; the guidance function is simply a full utilization of what should be part of the physical educator's expertise, namely the wide range of ways physical education can contribute to an individual's life. To sum up this contribution as carry-over sports and better health is a gross misrepresentation of the complexities of both the subject matter of physical education and the relevance of these activities for individual feelings and behavior.

In the area of needs, students may be counseled about observed behavior such as the need to win, the need for attention, or the need to feel pain. The guidance may be only bringing such matters to their attention or it may be asking their opinion of their behavior. Guidance in relation to interests may take the form of exploring possible untapped interests or encouraging students to try something new. Ability counseling involves both observations and analyses of test results and inquiries into a student's views of his own abilities. Whether a student wants to develop carry-over sport abilities or immediate achievements he can always remember can be a function of these guidance sessions. Finally, the relationships among needs, abilities, and interests must be explored for each student. For example, a student may be demonstrating a need to win in a recreational activity which is being played by others for fun, whereas his interests and abilities could suggest another activity wherein achievement is a common goal. To take this example a step further, the relationship between his current behavior in the recreational activity and the continuing opportunities for similar experiences in his life could be pointed out so that he could determine whether this is a meaningful way to act throughout his life.

Special projects can be designed which encourage introspection and thereby enhance self-understanding. One example, adapted from Fantini and Weinstein's curriculum of affect [6], is the time machine which projects the entire class ten or twenty years into the future. What the students see themselves doing in physical activity and what they feel about their past activities becomes the subject for discussion. A bulletin board confined to various accounts of people doing different kinds of activities and attaching different kinds of meanings would help not only by widening the options, but also by lending support to individual needs and interests. For example, *Sports Illustrated* recently carried an article on one of the top male ballet performers who was described as a great athlete [18], and stories of a wide variety of activities, from bicycling to lacrosse, which at least hold implications for a wide variety of needs, abilities, and interests have begun to appear regularly in magazines and even on sports pages. Stories of unusual feats, such as a record-breaking bench press by a 105 pound man or pictures of this year's Mr. America or of women engaged in vigorous sport are other possibilities for a self-understanding bulletin board.

## Interpersonal Relations

Despite the notion that value transfer must be a planned experience, learning is many times not a planned experience, because students learn in so many different ways. Therefore, an unplanned sport experience, because of the centrality of interaction, may well teach cooperation and sensitivity toward others, or it may teach opposing values. Having said this, we turn to methods for planning experiences which will enhance cooperation and sensitivity toward others both on and off the field. There are at least three approaches to achieving this goal.

The most formal approach is advocated by Sheehan and Alsop [32] and described briefly in the second and third chapters. To implement this method of instruction, teaching a team sport such as basketball would be expanded beyond the skill and strategy stage to include a block of time exclusively devoted to teaching the value under consideration—e.g., cooperation. The first part of the second stage would be a lecture and discussion of cooperation as it operates in basketball. Next, scrimmages would be held based on previously learned skills and strategies, but the instructor would use these scrimmages to point out the function of cooperation in basketball including on-the-floor examples of cooperation. Finally, the unit would conclude with a lecture and discussion of cooperation in society and how cooperation in basketball is related to cooperation in society. This approach requires time to be set aside for talking—which is bothersome to many physical educators —but Sheehan and Alsop argue that if we are really interested in "educational sport" we have no other choice.

Another approach which is particularly applicable to games and relays for young people involves observation of the extent of cooperation and sensitivity toward others exhibited during the activity, followed by a discussion of what happened and why in relation to these values. Some of my students have experimented with elementary school students by allowing them to choose or devise a game and, after the game, asking them to give their own analysis of "how it went." Invariably, the discussion turns to the question of whether the game was fun and, if it wasn't, why. Answers to why the game wasn't fun, especially if encouraged by the teacher, are anchored in discussions of both cooperation and the differing effects of the game on the players. At least at this age, before they are further inhibited from dealing with these kinds of issues, students are capable of recognizing the value of both cooperation and individual differences in a game situation.

Finally, it may be possible to teach cooperation and sensitivity toward others in an informal sport situation such as day camp volleyball or softball. Here the objective is to point out that sport can be fun without undue emphasis on winning, that the process of sport can have meaning apart from the product. This is a difficult goal, but it is a short step from this objective to a recognition that sport can be fun for others not as talented or as fortunate if only we can avoid making sport a miserable experience for others and instead develop an awareness of and sensitivity to their difficulties and help them toward a positive experience.

# References

1. AAHPER. *Organizational Patterns for Instruction in Physical Education.* Washington, D. C.: AAHPER, 1971.
2. Allen, Robert Eugene. "A Comparison of Personalized and Conventional Instruction in Men's Required Physical Education at the University of Florida." Unpublished doctoral dissertation, University of Florida, 1969.
3. Bloom, Benjamin S., ed. *Taxonomy of Educational Objectives: Handbook II, Affective Domain.* New York: David McKay Co., Inc., 1964.
4. Cohen, Stuart, and Hersh, Richard. "Behaviorism and Humanism: A Syn-

thesis for Teacher Education." *Journal of Teacher Education*, XXIII (Summer 1972), 172–76.

5. Dougherty, Neil Joseph. "A Comparison of the Effects of Command Task and Individual Program Styles of Teaching in the Development of Physical Fitness and Motor Skills." *Proceedings of the National College Physical Education Association for Men*, LXXIV (December 1970), 154–59.

6. Fantini, Mario, and Weinstein, Gerald, eds. *Toward Humanistic Education: A Curriculum of Affect.* New York: Praeger Publishers, Inc., 1970.

7. Farrell, Joan. "Programed vs. Teacher-Directed Instruction in Beginning Tennis for Women." *Research Quarterly*, XLI (March 1970), 51–57.

8. Gentile, A.M. "A Working Model for Skill Acquisition with Application to Teaching." *Quest*, XVII (January 1972), 3–23.

9. Glasser, William. *Schools Without Failure.* New York: Harper & Row, Publishers, 1969.

10. Goldberg, Miriam L.; Passow, A. Harry; and Justman, Joseph. *The Effects of Ability Grouping.* New York: Teachers College Press, 1966.

11. Hackett, Layne C., and Jenson, Robert G. *A Guide to Movement Exploration.* Rev. ed. Palo Alto, Calif.: Peek, 1967.

12. Hellison, Donald R. "Re-examining the Function of Interscholastic Athletics." *OAHPER Journal*, V (February 1971), 11ff.

13. Holt, John. *How Children Learn.* New York: Pitman Publishing Corp., 1967.

14. Jersild, Arthur T. *In Search of Self.* New York: Teachers College Press, 1952.

15. Keller, Roy Jacob. "A Comparison of Two Methods of Teaching Physical Education to Secondary School Boys." Unpublished doctoral dissertation, University of Illinois, 1963.

16. Kelley, Earle C. "The Place of Affective Learning." *Educational Leadership*, XXII (April 1965) 455–57.

17. Kephart, Newell C. *The Slow Learner in the Classroom.* Columbus: Charles E. Merrill Publishing Co., 1960.

18. Kram, Mark. "Encounter with an Athlete." *Sports Illustrated*, XXXV (September 27, 1971), 93–103.

19. Locke, Lawrence F., and Jensen, Mary. "Prepackaged Sports Skills Instruction: A Review of Selected Research." *JOHPER*, XLII (September 1971), 57–59.

20. Mager, Robert F. *Preparing Objectives for Programmed Instruction.* Belmont, Calif.: Fearon Publishers, 1962.

21. Manahan, Joan E. "Formulation of the Motor Plan." *Quest*, XVII (January 1972), 46–51.

22. Marburger, Donna Rae. "The Effect of Two Methods of Teaching Beginning Tennis on the Development of Tennis Skill and Knowledge and on Attitude Toward Physical Education." Unpublished doctoral dissertation, Colorado State University, 1965.

23. Mariani, Tom. "A Comparison of the Effectiveness of the Command Method and the Task Method of Teaching the Forehand and Backhand Tennis Strokes." *Reseach Quarterly,* XLI (May 1970), 171–74.

24. Mosston, Muska. *Teaching Physical Education: From Command to Discovery.* Columbus: Charles E. Merrill Publishing Co., 1966.

25. Mosston, Muska, and Mueller, Rudy. "Mission, Omission, and Submission in Physical Education." *Proceedings of the National Physical Education Association for Men,* LXXIII (December 1969), 122–30.

26. Nash, Robert J. "In the Summer of '71: An Experiment in Teacher Education." *Journal of Teacher Education,* XXIII (Spring 1972), 11–20.

27. Neill, A. S. *Summerhill: A Radical Approach to Child Rearing.* New York: Hart Publishing Co., Inc., 1960.

28. Pina, Wallace M. "The Systems Approach in Physical Education." *JOHPER,* XLII (November-December 1971), 57–58.

29. Schafer, Walter E., *et al.* "Programmed for Social Class: Tracking in High School." *Trans-action, VII* (October 1970), 39ff.

30. Seaman, Janet A. "Attitudes of Physically Handicapped Children Toward Physical Education." *Research Quarterly,* XLI (October 1970), 439–45.

31. Seefeldt, Vern. "Perceptual-Motor Skills." In *An Introduction to Measurement in Physical Education,* edited by Henry J. Montoye, Vol. 2, pp. 72–79. Indianapolis: Phi Epsilon Kappa Fraternity, 1970.

32. Sheehan, Thomas J., and Alsop, William L. "Educational Sport." *JOHPER,* XLIII (May 1972), 41–45.

33. "The New Physical Education." *JOHPER,* XLI (September 1971), 24–36.

34. Vodola, Thomas M. *Individualized Physical Education Program for the Handicapped Child.* Englewood Cliffs, N.J.: Prentice-Hall, Inc., 1973.

35. Weinberg, Carl, and Reidford, Philip. "Humanistic Educational Psychology." In *Humanistic Foundations of Education,* edited by Carl Weinberg, pp. 101–32. Englewood Cliffs, N.J.: Prentice-Hall, Inc., 1972.

36. Zeigler, Earle F., and VanderZwagg, H.J. *Physical Education: Progressivism or Essentialism?* Champaign, Ill.: Stipes Publishing Company, 1968.

# 7

# Summary

Social and emotional well-being has been an objective of some physical educators at least since the turn of the century, but the growth of humanism in recent years in concert with an increase in scholarly inquiry by the physical education profession has provided the opportunity for a fresh approach to behavioral development as a major concern of the profession. Vague discussions of the psycho-social benefits of the physical education experience as well as efforts to expand the body of knowledge of sport sociology and psychology have been replaced in this book by specific humanistic goals, methods to reach these goals, and a description of the difficulties involved in realizing these goals and methods in American society. The result is one physical educator's dream of a humanistic physical education.

From this perspective, four humanistic goals should guide the conduct of physical education. The first goal—self-esteem—refers to those feelings of competence or incompetence which derive from a person's subjective perceptions of his own experiences. An individual's self-esteem is an important beginning, because it forms the base of support for further behavioral development. Self-esteem may be specific to the ability or role under consideration or more general, in which case it could be influenced by feelings about specific abilities and roles. Physical education can contribute to an individual's base of support because physical ability—along with intellectual, social, and other abilities—is a dimension of everyone's potential behavior. A person's base of support is widened each time he feels competent about a particular motor skill or fitness activity or the capability of his body.

It is here, in the first step toward humanizing physical education, that the values of the American culture can be useful, because physical ability and appearance play an important part in the traditional value system of the American culture. Therefore, it is important in the beginning to provide success experiences which are socially approved, such as play experiences for children, courageous and aggressive activities for adolescent males, and feminine-oriented activities for adolescent females. The culture does not really facilitate self-esteem development; to the contrary, requirements that include boys proving themselves physically and girls proving their femininity only complicate and make more difficult the improvement of self-esteem for some individuals. Humanistic physical education can become a reality only if cultural values are loosened.

In addition to the value placed on physical ability and appearance, several other factors facilitate physical education's contribution to self-esteem development. The apparent relationship between how a person feels about his body and his self-esteem is one of these factors. Another involves the large and very visible affective component in physical education; it is difficult to come out of a physical activity experience free of some sort of feelings. Finally, the coach in organized sport can be a "significant other" in the life of his players and, as such, is in a key position to influence their feelings of physical competence or incompetence.

Critics of this approach have argued that by upgrading everyone's self-esteem we are creating a kind of leveling effect and will end up with a society that feels alike and behaves alike. However, the self-esteem goal is based upon the notion that each person is unique and has unique perceptions and feelings; elevating these feelings to the point that the individual feels comfortable with himself in no way means that everyone will feel alike. Further, feelings of self-worth are only a base of support for what follows; how a person behaves depends on myriad other factors.

Operating from a reasonably secure base of support, the individual can turn his attention to the second goal, self-actualization—that is, growth toward fulfillment of his special potentialities and talents. Any individual's potentialities span a wide range of abilities, including those within the province of physical education. The perspective developed in this book argues that one of physical education's tasks is to help people identify and develop specific physical abilities in line with their potentialities. For one person, it might be rope-skipping; for another, soccer skills and strategies; for a third, the development of a number of abilities. Good growth toward self-actualization may take place relatively early in life and become part of the individual's special memories and feelings, or it may be an ongoing process which the individual experiences throughout life.

Self-actualization also encompasses what Maslow has labeled "peak experiences," those moments of total involvement in an experience to which the person attaches his own meaning. Physical activity, like other experiences, contains the capacity for such total involvement, and the meanings that are derived from a particular physical activity experience range from joy and fun to the ascetic notion of pain and the courage to persevere under trying conditions. According to this view, the process is all-important; the product—i.e., winning—plays a secondary role. A third kind of self-actualization, which is often reserved for activities such as art and creative writing, involves physical activity as a potential form for creative self-expression, thus meeting the self-actualization requirement of moving beyond cultural confinements to full "beingness," awareness, and authenticity as a person. All three dimensions of self-actualization are anchored in positive feelings about the self so that the participant is free to become totally involved or to express himself without fear.

The quest for full self-actualization leads us to a third humanistic goal: self-understanding. If an individual's feelings and abilities are unique to him, he is in a better position, at least hypothetically, to determine what and how to learn. To profitably engage in this kind of introspection, however, requires considerable attention to the question "Who am I?" beyond those early efforts to establish a base of self-esteem ("Am I competent?"). He must be able to identify his needs and their sources (such as cultural values), his abilities, his interests, and the interrelationships among these variables. By understanding these components of the self, he can more readily integrate them into a meaningful life style which will bring him closer to social and emotional well-being. In physical education, this process is no less important than in other spheres of behavior. The needs that affect a person's feelings of competence, the potential abilities that he possesses, the meaning that physical activity could hold, the way to express himself through physical activity, the relationship of all of these things to each other and to past, present, and future behavior—answers to these kinds of questions constitute the essence of self-understanding in physical education.

The fourth and final humanistic goal moves beyond the self to social considerations. Although interpersonal relations are no doubt enhanced by feelings of self-worth, growth toward self-actualization, and self-understanding, the adoption of such values as sensitivity toward others and cooperation should further upgrade the quality of interpersonal relations, especially if the first three goals have already been met. Physical activity, especially sport, provides opportunities for interaction, and physical education programs could include intentional efforts to teach these values. Whether these values are specific to physical education or whether they instead transfer to interpersonal relations in the society has not yet been answered satisfactorily, although some evidence supports value transfer when it is specifically taught under certain conditions.

Although sensitivity toward others and, to a lesser extent, cooperation appear to be the antithesis of many traditional values—such as competition, aggressiveness, and courage—attributed to sport, they are not necessarily incompatible. Only when sport's interaction process is subverted by the war-oriented "win at all [or most] costs" product does a clear conflict of values arise. Otherwise, sport can and does serve a number of purposes without compromising any value orientations.

Humanism is often accused of being mystical, antiscientific, or, at best, philosophical in nature and therefore not amenable to proof or discreditation by "hard data" research. However, research in physical education has focused on some of the social-emotional outcomes of the physical education experience, and the results shed a little light on the feasibility of humanistic goals. While raising serious questions about character development in athletics and "burning off steam" as a justification for physical education programs in the schools, the evidence does, at least to some extent, uphold the self-esteem objective, and some of the data also support self-actualization and teaching values that apply to interpersonal relations.

An inspection of the majority of current physical education programs and individual patterns of physical activity strongly suggests that whatever contributions are being made to behavioral development are being made in the absence of humanistic goals. To be sure, humanistic goals have been achieved for some individuals both intentionally and accidentally within the current programs and activity patterns; but a concerted effort to help everyone reach these goals has not been characteristic of either American society or the physical education profession. The culture's influence is most apparent here, especially cultural value orientations such as competitive achievement and sex role characteristics which are perpetuated by the physical education profession, the family, and schools. Even religion has undermined humanistic goals by deprecating the body and play while glorifying the work ethic. Government's contribution has also been notably weak. In addition, minority groups have not been accorded equal opportunities to participate in the present system despite what appear to be unique needs for physical education experiences; as a result, some of the American people are denied full access to whatever behavioral development can be gained by taking part in physical education as it now exists.

Fortunately, there are signs of change. Some mechanisms for change, such as man's capacity for self-reflection, have always existed; others, such as the flexibility of the American society, have increased in recent years. American values appear to be shifting or at least loosening and humanistic thought is beginning to make its impact felt in a number of spheres. In sport, challenges are emerging, while the physical education profession has entered a period of serious scholarly inquiry, producing a proliferation of books and articles which may cause "grass roots" physical educators to think more about their own goals and methods.

If the conduct of physical education programs and the shape of physical activity patterns are to contribute systematically to social and emotional well-being, humanistic goals must be adopted and the present system must be amenable to change. But more than that, physical educators must become familiar with humanistic methods—that is, ways of achieving humanistic goals in physical education programs which will hopefully influence activity patterns as well. Humanistic methodology is based on the assumption that each student/participant is a unique person with unique talents and capacities who is potentially better able than anyone else to discern what is most meaningful for him and how he best learns. To bring these potentialities to fruition, he must be provided a wide range of opportunities within a nonthreatening environment and must progressively move from a structured style of teaching to a self-directed individualized approach, slowly shifting the responsibility for learning from the teacher to the student on an individual basis. Ultimately, if sufficient time were allotted, all students would accept full responsibility for planning, executing, and evaluating their own physical education programs.

Of course, implementation of these general guidelines require not only time but specific methods. Self-esteem can be facilitated in a number of ways: teacher behavior can communicate the "specialness" of each student; subject matter can be selected which provides ample opportunities for success; the facility can be arranged so that there are private places to try things out; and policies concerning clothing, showers, and the like can be altered to suit individual needs. To assist the self-actualization process, curriculum planning is necessary, including perceptual-motor and fundamental motor skill screening and individual help, opportunities for self-expressive activities, a wide variety of experiences, specialization, a sound measurement program designed to help students identify their potentialities, and a knowledge base to facilitate self-development. The development of self-understanding, so necessary if students are to eventually plan their own programs, can be encouraged both by group guidance meetings aimed at typical needs, interests, and the integration of these into a life style, and by individual guidance sessions tailored to the uniqueness of the individual. Sensitivity toward others and cooperation, as values central to interpersonal relations, can be caught accidentally as a result of group interaction in sport, but intentional planning either using problem-solving or by directly teaching toward these values holds more promise for exposing students to these values and their connection to society.

The success of these goals and methods depends not only on the adoption of humanistic physical education as one physical educator's perspective, but on the implementation of humanistic physical education programs at all levels and, to be even more complete, on a wide ranging interrelated set of programs both in and outside physical education. Only then will the influences described in this book be assured some certainty of taking hold. However, one humanistic program—a few weeks or months in someone's life—may bring a few individuals closer to social and emotional well-being. We must start somewhere.

# Index

*115*